WESTLAKE HIGH SCHOOL
99N 200 W
SARATOGA SPRINGS,

MW01078324

Selma and the Voting Rights Act

SELMA AND THE VOTING RIGHTS ACT

David Aretha

MORGAN REYNOLDS

PUBLISHING

Greensboro, North Carolina

THE CIVIL RIGHTS MOVEMENT

The Trial of the Scottsboro Boys
Marching in Birmingham
Selma and the Voting Rights Act
The Murder of Emmett Till
Freedom Summer

SELMA AND THE VOTING RIGHTS ACT

Copyright © 2008 by David Aretha

Library of Congress Cataloging-in-Publication Data

Aretha, David.
  Selma and the Voting Rights Act / by David Aretha. -- 1st ed.
      p. cm. -- (Civil rights series)
  Includes bibliographical references and index.
  ISBN-13: 978-1-59935-056-1
  ISBN-10: 1-59935-056-4
  1. Selma (Ala.)--Race relations--History--20th century--Juvenile literature. 2. Selma-Montgomery Rights March, 1965--Juvenile literature. 3. King,
Martin Luther, Jr., 1929-1968--Juvenile literature. 4. African Americans--Civil
rights--Alabama--Selma--History--20th century--Juvenile literature. 5. Civil
rights movements--Alabama--Selma--History--20th century--Juvenile literature. 6. African Americans--Suffrage--Alabama--Selma--History--20th cen-
tury--Juvenile literature. 7. United States. Voting Rights Act of 1965--Juvenile
literature. I. Title.
  F334.S4A74 2007
  324.6'208996073--dc22

                                                  2007024655

Printed in the United States of America
First Edition

Contents

Voting rights activists marching from Selma to Montgomery
(*Library of Congress*)

one

White Voters Only

Reverend C. T. Vivian had reached his boiling point. For weeks in 1965, Vivian and the Southern Christian Leadership Conference (SCLC) had tried to help the black citizens of Selma, Alabama, register to vote, but Dallas County Sheriff Jim Clark would not allow it. The flagrantly racist lawman had broken up numerous demonstrations outside the courthouse, ordering the arrests of several thousand African Americans, including hundreds of children. Clark and his deputies cracked protesters with nightsticks and stung them with electric cattle prods as they marched them off to jail.

Since 1868, African Americans had possessed the constitutional right to vote. But through much of the segregated South, whites suppressed that right with racist laws, incessant intimidation, and downright refusal to allow black citizens to register to vote. Whites held all the power in the South, and they were not about to give it up.

On February 16, 1965, Reverend Vivian and other black demonstrators climbed the steps of the county courthouse in Selma. Amid a steady rain and surrounded by armed deputies and reporters, the group attempted to enter the courthouse—only to be denied personally by Clark. A fed-up Vivian turned and addressed the deputies.

"We want you to know, gentlemen, that—every one of you—we know your badge numbers, we know your names. . . . There are those who followed Hitler like you blindly follow this Sheriff Clark. . . . You're racists in the same way Hitler was a racist."

Local whites could not believe they were hearing this from a black man. Traditionally in the South, before the civil rights movement began in earnest just a few years earlier, blacks could be punished simply for not saying "sir" to a white man or for "eyeballing" a white woman. Vivian, in their minds, had drastically crossed the line, yet he kept on talking.

"You can't keep anyone in the U.S. from voting without hurting the rights of all other citizens," Vivian said. "Democracy's built on this. This is why every man has the right to vote. . . . And this is what we're trying to say to you. These people have the right to stand inside this courthouse. If you'd had your basic civics courses, you'd know this, gentlemen."

At that point, Clark ordered all television cameramen to turn off their lights. He then reared back and socked Vivian in the mouth, sending the reverend tumbling down the stone steps. The sheriff broke his own finger, but to him it was worth it. The punch was a potent warning symbol: As long as Sheriff Clark was on watch, African Americans would not have equal rights in Selma, Alabama.

C. T. Vivian (left) leads a prayer as Sheriff James Clark (right) stops Vivian and other protesters from entering the Selma courthouse. *(Courtesy of AP Images)*

Although President Lincoln had "freed" the slaves with his Emancipation Proclamation in 1863, blacks were still subservient to whites 102 years later—especially in the "Jim Crow" segregated South. The Thirteenth Amendment (1865) had abolished slavery and involuntary servitude, and the Fifteenth Amendment (1870) had guaranteed voting rights to all adult male citizens. (American women were granted voting rights in 1920.) Southern whites, however, resisted black equality from the get-go.

In the late 1800s, southern legislatures began to systematically deprive blacks of equal rights. "Jim Crow" became a euphemism for segregation in the South—a system that would remain firmly entrenched up through the 1950s. In this segregated society, whites had their own facilities and blacks had theirs—which were almost always inferior to whites'.

Many southern whites wanted to keep African Americans oppressed. For one thing, they wanted to maintain blacks as cheap labor—for example, field hands who would continue to work for pitiful wages.

Moreover, many whites believed African Americans were subhuman, unworthy of equal rights. Also, many whites feared the sexual consequences of integration, believing that "black bucks" would breed with "white maidens" and produce "mongrel" children. In 1892, South Carolina Governor Ben Tillman said, "Governor as I am, I would lead a mob to lynch the Negro who ravishes a white woman."

In the South (and in some northern locales), whites passed numerous laws to keep African Americans "in their place." Blacks were forced to use separate railway cars, drinking fountains, and public restrooms. Whites called a black man "boy," but blacks had to call a white man "Mister." An African American had to step off the sidewalk when encountering a white person. And if a black man even looked at an attractive white woman, he could be arrested for what was called "reckless eyeballing." Alarmingly harsh sentences were administered to blacks who broke laws—even the bogus laws that southern legislatures had created. Many African Americans were killed for the slightest violations—or just for being black.

In 1876, the U.S. Supreme Court struck a hard blow to the Fifteenth Amendment, stating that the amendment did not *guarantee* citizens the right to vote. The High Court listed the grounds impermissible for denying the vote, which indirectly gave southern states ways to disenfranchise black voters.

In 1890, Mississippi led southern states in amending their constitutions to exclude most blacks from voting. Whites feared that if African Americans voted in large numbers, they might elect black leaders, since in many communities, blacks outnumbered whites.

Southern legislatures concocted many schemes to deny the vote, even into the 1960s. They made aspiring voters pay poll taxes (which were too expensive for poor blacks) and prove their literacy (many blacks were illiterate due to poor economic conditions and inferior public schools). White voting registrars made applicants pass extremely difficult civics tests to "earn" the right to vote. A sample question on one test was: "The power of granting patents . . . is given to the Congress for the purpose of _____?" (Answer: promoting progress.)

Most whites could not answer such questions, but southern registrars often didn't give such tests to whites. Or the registrars helped them answer the questions, or they passed a white applicant and failed a black applicant even if they had posted the same score. Frequently, registrars simply never notified blacks if their registration application was approved or rejected.

Said Nicholas Katzenbach, U.S. attorney general in the mid-1960s, "The problem in the South was primarily the problem of literacy tests [a short-hand term for all the pre-registration tests] and the way in which they were administered. You had black Ph.D.'s who couldn't pass a literacy test and you had whites who could barely write their name who had no problem being registered to vote."

Even if an African American registered, he or she might never get to cast a ballot. Blacks were known to be threatened, beaten, and even killed for trying to vote. More common was economic intimidation. Whites often fired or refused to hire blacks who voted or registered to vote. A white community could put the squeeze on a black voter; for example, refuse to sell him supplies for his farm. Against such enormous roadblocks, few African Americans in the South even tried to register. In 1940, only 3 percent of southern blacks were registered to vote, and the numbers were worse in Alabama and Mississippi—0.4 percent in each.

In the first half of the 20th century, the National Association for the Advancement of Colored People (NAACP) led the push for civil rights. But in Washington—where white men dominated Congress, the Supreme Court, and presidential administrations—only the most liberal politicians cared about black causes. This especially was true during the Great Depression of the 1930s and during World War II.

In 1944, hope for African Americans arrived with a Supreme Court decision. In *Smith v. Allwright,* the court ruled that black citizens no longer could be excluded from voting in political party primary elections. With this trick removed from their bag, southern legislators searched for other ways to disenfranchise African Americans. In 1946, for example, Alabama approved the Boswell Amendment. It stated that prospective voters had to read, write, explain the Constitution, demonstrate an understanding of the duties and obligations of citizenship, prove they possessed "good character," and prove they had been regularly employed over the past year. (This amendment soon was ruled unconstitutional.)

The national civil rights movement began in earnest in 1955. The lynching of Emmett Till, a fourteen-year-old African American from Chicago, in Mississippi sparked a firestorm of upset among

African Americans and many northern whites. The subsequent trial illustrated another consequence of disenfranchisement. In Mississippi, only registered voters could serve on juries. That resulted in an all-white jury in the Till trial, and it voted to acquit Till's killers in a blatant case of racism. Also in 1955, the famed bus boycott in Montgomery, Alabama, began in December. Reverend Martin Luther King Jr. led the local—and

Emmett Till *(Library of Congress)*

soon regional—fight against segregation.

Though President Dwight Eisenhower seemed indifferent to the cause, Congress did pass a civil rights act in 1957. Sections of this law related to voting. The 1957 act stated that if the U.S. attorney general believed a registrar was denying a citizen's right to vote, the attorney general had the authority to file a civil suit in a federal district court.

That aspect of the 1957 Civil Rights Act proved pitifully ineffective. Few voting-injustice cases ever went to court, as southern blacks (who were mostly rural) were largely unaware of their legal right to file a lawsuit. Even fewer African Americans were willing to go to such extraordinary lengths—and risk white retaliation—just to cast a single vote.

Moreover, the U.S. Justice Department and Civil Rights Commission struggled to get voting rights cases started. At the outset of such cases, they needed to obtain registration and voting records from southern registrars, who typically were uncooperative. On dozens of occasions, registrars refused to supply such records.

Even if a voting rights case got to court, it still faced an uphill battle. Though the cases were tried in federal courts, the trials were held in the South, and the judges—though appointed by the president—were southern. And many southern judges were segregationists.

In 1960, Congress passed another civil rights act, which also included sections about voting rights. The new legislation mandated that registrars preserve their registration and voting records, and it stated that the Justice Department had the right to examine those records upon demand. It also stated that in certain instances a federal judge could appoint a voting referee to reexamine voter applicants who had been rejected by county registrars. In practice, though, these new stipulations had little impact.

Statistics prove just how ineffective the 1957 and 1960 civil rights acts were. From 1956 to 1962, the number of voting-age blacks registered to vote rose from 25 percent to a still paltry 29 percent. In Alabama, the percentage rose from eleven to just thirteen—and this was during the heart of the civil rights movement.

Extraordinary events in 1963 convinced Congress to pass even more civil rights legislation. That spring, Martin Luther King led a campaign to end segregation in Birmingham, Alabama. When city officials attacked black demonstrators with fire hoses and police dogs, the nation demanded justice. On August 28, a quarter-million Americans marched on Washington and heard King deliver his immortal "I Have a Dream" speech. The day galvanized most of America in support of civil rights. Afterward, President John F. Kennedy urged Congress to pass what would become the Civil Rights Act of 1964.

The 1964 act would prove effective in dismantling segregation, but not in guaranteeing voting rights. The new

Martin Luther King delivers his "I Have A Dream Speech" to a crowd in Washington, D.C. *(Courtesy of the Department of Defense)*

law did state that voting rights cases would be handled by a special three-judge district court (so that a single segregationist judge could not sabotage a case). It also stated that registration standards should be applied uniformly, that no one's registration application could be rejected due to minor errors, that only written literacy tests could be used, and that a sixth-grade education was good enough presumption of literacy. But the 1964 act still did not address the central problem regarding voting rights: that the only way to overcome voting injustice was to file a lawsuit.

Lyndon B. Johnson, who assumed the presidency after Kennedy was assassinated in November 1963, understood what needed to be done regarding voting rights. The law needed to state that federal officials could register voters in locales where African Americans were disenfranchised. But with the latest act signed on July 2, 1964, it seemingly would be a long time before Congress would consider more civil rights legislation.

In the early 1960s, some gains were made in registering southern black voters—not due to federal legislation but because of the grassroots efforts of black activists. Such organizations as the Student Nonviolent Coordinating Committee (SNCC) and the Southern Regional Council took active roles in registering voters. Volunteers went door-to-door, urging blacks to register and explaining how to do so.

Due largely to such efforts, black registration did increase substantially in the South—up to 43 percent by 1964. But in states of great resistance, the numbers remained low in 1964. Alabama stood at 23 percent and Mississippi less than 7 percent.

In 1964, SNCC leader Robert Moses organized "Freedom Summer," in which volunteers (including many northern white college students) tried to register rural African Americans. Not only were their efforts largely unsuccessful, with only a small fraction of voter applications approved by registrars, but white Mississippians responded with acts of terror: shootings, beatings, and bombings. The FBI was called in, but it hurt more than helped the civil rights cause. Headed by staunch right-winger J. Edgar Hoover, the FBI focused on civil rights activists (including King), whom the bureau considered "agitators" and potential threats to society.

By August 1964, when the bodies of three Freedom Summer volunteers were found shot to death outside Philadelphia, Mississippi, it was clear that grassroots registration efforts weren't the total solution to the voting problem. Martin Luther King and the SCLC believed that they needed to showcase voting injustice with another movement, one that would cause a national uproar and force another, more powerful bill through Congress. Their first step was to choose a city to stage the drama.

two

Demanding the Ballot

SCLC leaders didn't need to argue about where to stage their voting rights campaign. In fact, the name of the ideal city was immediately apparent: *Selma, Alabama,* located fifty-four miles west of Montgomery near the dead center of the state.

Selma in 1964 boasted a population of 29,500—14,400 whites and 15,100 blacks. Despite being outnumbered, whites ruled the city. Moreover, their control of the voting registration office ensured their political power. Despite all the civil rights legislation passed in recent years, 99 percent of Selma's registered voters were white. In Dallas County, only fourteen African Americans had been added to the voting rolls from 1954 to 1961.

Prior to 1965, Selma had been a civil rights battleground for several years. On the grassroots level, SNCC workers Bernard and Colia Lafayette initiated the Dallas County Voters' League in Selma in February 1963. Each month thereafter, dozens of

Map of Alabama
(Courtesy of the National Atlas)

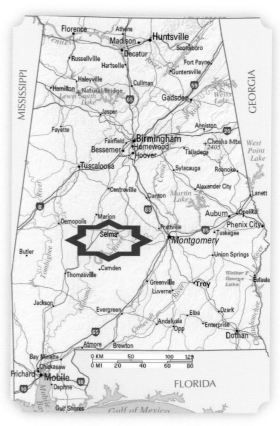

aspiring black voters attended SNCC-sponsored meetings in Dallas County. But, because of arrests and fear of retaliation by local whites (including employers), African Americans stopped attending the meetings, and they were soon discontinued.

On October 7, 1963, SNCC led a large march of protesters to the county courthouse in Selma. Dallas County sheriff Jim Clark, his deputies, and his posse (volunteers, many of whom belonged to the Ku Klux Klan) broke up the protest. In fact, the lawmen even beat those who tried to bring food and water to those in line. SNCC leader John Lewis recalled that "hundreds of people lined up and stood at the county courthouse for most of the day, and at the end of the day only about five people had made it in to take the so-called literacy tests." SNCC's campaign fizzled out after that, having garnered little national publicity.

John Lewis, national chairman of SNCC
(Courtesy of AP Images)

The U.S. Justice Department devoted much of its attention to Dallas County. In fact, the Justice Department filed more voting rights suits in Selma than in any other city. The first, in 1961, was delayed by segregationist Judge Daniel Thomas, who eventually denied relief to the plaintiff. When the Justice Department moved for a restraining order against Sheriff Clark and others in November 1963, Thomas again held firm.

Black community activists formed the Dallas County Improvement Association in 1963. They aimed to remove the "White" and "Colored" signs from public buildings, investigate police brutality against blacks, and improve access to jobs and voter registration. Selma officials ignored the organization's concerns.

The SNCC was back in Selma in summer 1964. But on July 5, Clark's men broke up a voter registration rally with nightsticks and tear gas. As Lewis and fifty African Americans were marched to the courthouse the next day, they were stung with electric prods and rushed to jail.

Thanks to Sheriff Clark and Judge Thomas, whites successfully defended their supremacy in Selma. By fall 1964, only several hundred blacks were registered in Dallas County even though, said John Doar of the Justice Department, "the litigation method of correction has been tried harder here than anywhere else in the South."

Courts clearly were not the answer to solving voting injustice. As stated in a *Virginia Law Review* article by Barry E. Hawk and John J. Kirby Jr., "The patience of the nation with the judicial process ran out in Selma, Alabama."

In late December 1964, a Selma committee in conjunction with the Dallas County Voters' League formally invited Martin Luther King to Selma to help them procure the right to vote. But they did not have to ask, as King and the SCLC—beginning in November '64—already were targeting Selma as the next battleground in the civil rights movement, with voting rights being the central issue.

King knew that Selma was the perfect city to showcase injustice. Not only were the voting registration numbers alarming, but Clark—with his hot temper and short fuse—was the ideal villain for a civil rights morality play. The SCLC's 1962 campaign in Albany, Georgia, had fallen flat when Police Chief Laurie Pritchett treated black protesters with respect. But the Birmingham campaign in 1963 had been a rousing success due to Public Safety Director Bull Connor's hostile treatment of protesters—which was televised nationally. The SCLC needed another Bull Connor, and Clark was it.

"They picked Selma just like a movie producer picked a set," said Selma Mayor Joseph Smitherman. "You had the right ingredients. I mean, you would've had to seen Clark in his day. He had a helmet like General Patton.

He had the clothes, the Eisenhower jacket, and the swagger stick."

Andrew Young, the SCLC's young executive director, added: "Jim Clark was a near madman. It just infuriated him for anybody to defy his authority, even when they just wanted to vote. If he said you couldn't vote, you were supposed to go away. And just to stand there enraged him."

Late in 1964, Mayor Smitherman commissioned Selma's public safety director, Wilson Baker, to ask federal officials to prevent Martin Luther King from coming to Selma. Smitherman was a young, slender, low-key "moderate"— although still a segregationist. He was trying to attract industries to Selma, and he knew that a massive protest campaign would be a public relations disaster.

Sheriff Jim Clark *(Courtesy of AP Images)*

The Johnson administration did not try to prevent King's visit to Selma. In fact, in late 1964, President Johnson asked Attorney General Nicholas Katzenbach to draft a proposal for voting rights—although not to make it public. President Johnson figured that Congress and the nation needed time to "digest" the 1964 Civil Rights Act, and that congress-men (especially those from southern states) might mount vocal opposition to a new bill brought forth soon after the last one.

Still, in January the federal government was supporting the movement. In his State of the Union Address on January 4, President Johnson said, "I propose that we eliminate every remaining obstacle to the right and the opportunity to vote." On January 8, the Justice Department completed a draft of a proposed constitutional amendment, and a week later the department filed suit against Alabama's statewide registra-tion test.

The drama in Selma began on January 2, 1965. While Clark was out of town, King checked in at the historic Hotel Albert, becoming the first African American ever to do so. A white segregationist, James Robinson, greeted the recent Nobel Peace Prize winner by punching him twice in the face and aiming two kicks at his groin. Robinson was hustled off to jail.

That day, King spoke to a packed house of seven hun-dred at Selma's Brown Chapel African Methodist Episcopal Church. He outlined the SCLC's mission in the city. If Dallas County officials did not register large numbers of African Americans, he said, there would be enormous street demon-strations in Selma. "If appeals to the state government were denied," King intoned, "we will seek to arouse the federal

King stands in front of the Hotel Albert in Selma. *(Courtesy of AP Images/ Bill Hudson)*

government by marching by the thousands [to] the places of registration." He demanded, "Give us the ballot!"

While King's speech roused the citizens of Selma, SNCC's leadership was not enthused. Many SNCC members, who were still trying to register black voters in Dallas County, resented King's arrival. They believed he exploited certain cities (such as Albany, Birmingham, and now Selma) to make a national statement, then left without any real progress made in such cities. Regarding Albany in 1962, wrote Taylor Branch, SNCC leaders "charged that he [King] skimmed publicity off their groundwork." SNCC's resentment of King and the SCLC would flare up throughout the Selma campaign.

Regardless, King and the SCLC moved forward with their plans. Although they proclaimed a philosophy of nonviolent protest, in keeping with the example set by India's Mohandas Gandhi, their strategy was to subtly provoke lawmen into mistreating and abusing protesters, as in Birmingham. The goal was to garner empathy: to be viewed by Americans (through the media) as noble victims. King was smart enough not to explain the strategy publicly, since it would come across as contriving. Moreover, the strategy of deliberately putting black citizens, sometimes children, in harm's way would not sit well. Instead, the SCLC's stated goal was to, basically, march for justice.

SCLC leaders could defend their strategy by saying it was the only plan that worked. Moreover, provoking a little violence paled in comparison to the three-hundred year crime of slavery and Jim Crow. And besides, they truly *were* marching for justice.

Unable to keep King from coming, Smitherman and the city administration aimed to put on a good face. On the day King arrived, seven of Selma's restaurants were quietly integrated. Even Clark—on orders from above—kept his cool on the day of the first large SCLC demonstration, January 18.

King proceeded to lead more than four hundred African Americans to the county courthouse to register to vote. Most were rounded up by Clark's men and roped off in an alley. Despite the presence of the American Nazi Party, no violence ensued—but no one was registered.

The next day Reverend Ralph Abernathy of the SCLC (King's right-hand man) led another march to the courthouse—only

Rev. Fred Shuttlesworth (left), Rev. Ralph Abernathy (middle), and Martin Luther King (right) lead a group of African Americans toward the Selma courthouse during a voter registration drive. *(Library of Congress)*

this time the participants refused to be herded into the alley. Clark responded with sixty-six arrests. Amelia Boynton, a leader of the Dallas County Voters' League who had been trying to help blacks register for years, was slow to follow orders.

"She's an educated woman," said Evelyn Gibson Lowery, a fellow activist. "She was able to correct the registrars. She would tell them how to pronounce words." The registrars didn't like Boynton, nor did Clark. When she wouldn't follow orders, he grabbed her by the collar and pushed her roughly to a patrol car a half block away. Photos of the incident were published in newspapers nationwide the next day. It was precisely the type of publicity the SCLC was seeking.

On January 22, more than one hundred black schoolteachers marched to the courthouse to protest Boynton's arrest. It

Annie Lee Cooper struggles with Sheriff Jim Clark (center) and his deputies during her beating and arrest. *(Courtesy of AP Images)*

was a courageous act by the educators—they risked serious retaliation by the white school board. After being jabbed and pushed down the courthouse steps by lawmen, the teachers returned to Brown Chapel, where they were cheered for their efforts.

Even Daniel Thomas, the segregationist federal judge, helped the cause. On January 23, he issued a temporary restraining order preventing Selma and Dallas County officials from interfering with voting registration efforts—although he did limit courthouse assemblies to one hundred protesters.

On January 25, a fifty-three-year-old hotel manager named Annie Lee Cooper threw the most publicized punch since boxer Cassius Clay had pummeled Sonny Liston a year earlier. During a courthouse march that day, she told

Clark, "Ain't nobody scared around here." Clark responded by shoving her, and Cooper retaliated with a punch to Clark's head that knocked him down. Deputies then held Cooper on the ground while Clark beat her repeatedly with his nightstick. "Clark whacked her so hard," said SNCC leader John Lewis, "we could hear the sound several rows back."

Cooper explained the incident in detail: "They wrestled me to the ground. He [Clark] got up in my stomach with his knees and he hit me over my eye with his billy club. . . . He was in my stomach and I couldn't move because there were three of them. . . . Some of the [demonstrators] started to rage and wanted to fight. And Dr. King told them to be calm, be calm. No fighting, no fighting."

The next day, a photo of Clark clubbing Cooper made page one of the *New York Times*.

After several days of relative calm, King arrived in Selma again on January 31. The next day, he spoke to marchers before they headed to the courthouse. "If Negroes could vote, there would be no Jim Clarks," he preached, "there would be no oppressive poverty directed against Negroes, our children would not be crippled by segregated schools, and the whole community might live together in harmony."

From there, the Selma movement intensified. On a march to the courthouse that day, King and 250 protesters were arrested for exceeding the one hundred-person limit. But this was what King wanted. While others were freed on bond, King and Ralph Abernathy decided to make a statement by remaining in jail. Later that day, about five hundred school children in Selma were arrested during a mass demonstration. And in nearby Marion, Alabama, six hundred people protested.

Children singing as they march toward a detention center after being arrested outside the courthouse in Selma *(Library of Congress)*

Believing it was worth it to go to jail for justice, hundreds more African Americans were taken into custody on February 2. The next day, three hundred-plus young people in Selma and more than seven hundred protesters in Marion were taken into custody. On February 5, five hundred more were arrested in a courthouse gathering. Spirits among African Americans ran high all week, as they sang the civil rights anthem "We Shall Overcome." Clark, meanwhile, wore a button that read "Never!"

The massive arrests overwhelmed everyone from Selma to Washington. Many white citizens in town felt that Clark was out of control, while local business owners complained about plummeting sales due to the chaos in the streets. Prisoners in makeshift jails fared worse, stating that they were being denied proper water, food, and bedding.

While in jail, King wrote a letter dated February 1 that was printed as an advertisement in the *New York Times* four days later. "Why are we in jail?" he wrote. "Have you ever been required to answer 100 questions on government, some abstruse even to a political science specialist, merely to vote? Have you ever stood in line with over a hundred others and after waiting an entire day seen less than ten given the qualifying test? This is Selma, Alabama. There are more Negroes in jail with me than there are on the voting rolls."

On February 4, the charismatic Malcolm X made a brief appearance in Selma. Normally a harsh critic of nonviolent protest—thinking it a meek response to white oppression—he gave a surprisingly mild speech at Brown Chapel and shortly left town. (Seventeen days later, he would be assassinated by members of the Nation of Islam, with which he had had a falling out.)

Meanwhile, the commotion in Selma sparked politicians into action. On February 4, Judge Thomas ordered Dallas Country registrars to discontinue the "knowledge of government" test, to not reject applicants due to minor errors, and to process at least one hundred applicants on each day that the board met. If all applicants were not processed by July, Thomas stated, he would appoint a referee.

In Washington, fifteen congressmen, including black Representative Charles Diggs (D-MI), left for Selma to get a firsthand account of the injustice. Senator Jacob Javits called the hundreds of arrests "shocking." He added that the Selma situation "may well show that federal legislation is required authorizing the appointment of federal registrars who would themselves be empowered to register citizens to vote."

On February 4, President Johnson met with the White House press corps and addressed the Selma situation in broad terms. He concluded his prepared statement by saying: "I hope that all Americans will join me in expressing their concern in the loss of any American's right to vote. Nothing is more fundamental to American citizenship and to our freedom as a nation and as a people. I intend to see that the right is secured for all our citizens."

Meanwhile, back in Selma, King left jail on February 5, and announced the Selma campaign would be accelerated even further. He was half right. Arrests would diminish, but tensions would be on the rise. On February 8, the SCLC's James Bevel tried to enter the courthouse, only to be shoved down the steps by a furious Clark, who fumed, "You're making a mockery out of justice." Clark then had Bevel and fifty others arrested.

That same day, Representatives John Lindsay and Joseph Resnick of New York introduced their own voting rights bills. Representative Bradford Morse of Massachusetts summarized the growing feeling on Capitol Hill: "I had hoped that we could wait until we had an opportunity to see the [1964] Civil Rights Act in operation before we took up new legislation, but the events of recent weeks have made this impossible."

The next day, nineteen representatives talked on the House floor about voting rights. Down the road, King met with Vice President Hubert Humphrey for an hour and a half and President Johnson for fifteen minutes. Later, King informed the press, "The President made it very clear to me that he was determined during his administration to see all remaining obstacles removed to the right of Negroes to vote."

King (right) meets with President Johnson. *(Courtesy of the Lyndon Baines Johnson Library)*

While King had the president in his corner, Clark had plenty of fight left. On February 10, 160 students staged a quiet demonstration outside the courthouse. Though they did not shout, they did pull out small signs, one of which said "Jim Clark Is a Cracker." In what historian Taylor Branch called a game of "hide the demonstrators," Clark ordered two buses to be stationed between the protesters and the press. The students responded by breaking up into two groups. After a meeting in the courthouse, Clark emerged with a new plan.

"Move out!" he barked to the young demonstrators. Clark and his deputies lined up the students single file on Alabama Avenue, then led them on a march toward the outskirts of the city. Responding to a student who had asked where they were going, a deputy said, "You wanted to march, didn't you?"

Gradually, the walk evolved into a trot, with deputies prodding the students with electric cattle prods and whacks from their billy clubs. Before long, the lawmen simply chased the scared protesters while Clark and others rode along in cars.

Two miles up River Road, Clark positioned a rear guard to block the press. The forced march lasted for several miles before the students dispersed and the lawmen gave up the chase. Some of the protesters—winded and frightened—bent over and vomited.

The forced march of minors angered many of Selma's white citizens. The *Selma Times-Journal* condemned the action, while Public Safety Director Wilson Baker said he would arrest Clark himself if he did something like that again. On February 11, Clark laid low—making no arrests—as six hundred marched to the courthouse. The same day, Congressman Diggs and others telegrammed the president, urging that the administration draft a bill to ensure voting rights and eliminate literacy tests and poll taxes.

Little happened from Friday, February 12 through Valentine's Day, though Clark was hospitalized for exhaustion. On Monday, February 15, the Justice Department reported that a constitutional amendment would not be a satisfactory approach to the voting rights problem, meaning legislation would be better.

That day in Selma, one of only two days during the month in which voting registration was open, a record 1,500 people lined up to register. The line was literally a mile long, stretching nearly ten blocks. By day's end, only ninety people completed applications to register, while four hundred others signed an "appearance book" that allegedly secured them a future place in the registration line.

It was on February 16 that Clark punched Reverend Vivian after his historic speech on the courthouse steps. Over the next two days, attitudes soured on both sides. Even those Selma whites who disliked Clark were losing their patience with black protesters and their seemingly never-ending marches. The *Selma Times-Journal* stated that King and "outside forces" had pushed "all sound-thinking citizens perilously near the breaking point."

Meanwhile, King was growing frustrated with the lack of success within Selma: relatively few African Americans had yet to be registered to vote. Though feeling ill, King managed to speak at Brown Chapel on Wednesday evening. "Selma *still* isn't right," he intoned. "We must engage in broader civil disobedience to bring the attention of the nation on Dallas County. It may well be that we might have to march out of this church at night."

The prospect of a night march frightened many people. To disrupt the quiet of the evening with a provocative march would surely anger white citizens. Moreover, blacks would be more vulnerable to attack during the dark of night.

All the while, whites were growing more hostile. That same Wednesday night, whites in Marion gathered to discuss how to handle the black protesters. When two white meeting-goers suggested negotiations, they were verbally and physically assaulted.

Tensions were rising on both sides. Without some kind of relief, it wouldn't be long until the community snapped.

three

Bloody Selma

With tensions high in Marion on Thursday, February 18, officials called in Alabama state troopers. That morning, sheriff's deputies arrested the SCLC's James Orange for contributing to the delinquency of young marchers. Reacting to the arrest, Albert Turner of the Perry County Voters League asked Reverend C. T. Vivian to speak at Mount Zion Baptist Church in Marion that evening. Hundreds showed up.

After Vivian's address to the packed church, the congregation began a march to the jail. It was less than a half-block away, and their plan was simply to sing a "freedom song" and then head home. Yet it was a night march (9:30 p.m.), and fifty state troopers and a band of seething white townspeople stopped them before they reached the jail. Police Chief T. O. Harris ordered the marchers to return to the church or disperse. When Reverend James Dobynes responded instead by kneeling in prayer, he was clubbed on the head by a state trooper and dragged by two men to the jail.

Suddenly, troopers began to attack African Americans. Many of the marchers ran back toward Mount Zion Baptist, only to run into throngs of people still leaving the church. Reporters, who had been restricted to the town square, ran toward the action. Whites responded by roughing up two photographers and demolishing their cameras. Others sprayed the lenses of cameras with black aerosol paint.

NBC News correspondent Richard Valeriani was whacked on the head with an ax handle. A state trooper responded by confiscating the weapon but not arresting the perpetrator. Valeriania recalled:

> Then another white man walked up to me and said, "Are you hurt? Do you need a doctor?" I was stunned, and I put my hand on the back of my head and it was full of blood. I said to him, "Yeah, I think I do. I'm bleeding." And then he thrust his face right up against mine and said, "Well, we don't have doctors for people like you."

With congestion around the church doors, many protesters ran for safety in nearby buildings. Troopers, said Albert Turner, "beat people at random. They didn't have to be marching. All you had to do was be black." One person even clubbed the skull of eighty-two-year-old Cager Lee, who—while bleeding—ran into nearby Mack's Cafe. There he spotted his daughter, Viola Jackson, and grandson, Jimmie Lee Jackson, but the violence and chaos wasn't over yet.

Some troopers forced marchers into the cafe, then wreaked total havoc. They overturned tables, smashed lights, and attacked the protesters. In the kitchen, troopers attacked

Cager Lee again. When his daughter ran to protect him, she was thrown to the floor and beaten. Jimmie Lee went to protect her, only to be shoved by a trooper against a cigarette machine. Then, someone shot Jimmie Lee twice in the stomach. Still not finished, whites continued to club him until he collapsed outside. Jimmie Lee Jackson and nine others were hospitalized, while other beaten marchers were hauled off to jail.

The next day, February 19, church services were held all day in Marion for the recovery of Jackson, who clung to life at Good Samaritan Hospital in Selma. Twenty-six years old, Jackson was a pulpwood worker and a deacon at Saint James Baptist Church. Even though he was a high school graduate and had served his country in Vietnam, Jackson had been turned down when he applied to register to vote—not just once, but five times.

On the 19th, Martin Luther King exhorted Attorney General Nicholas Katzenbach to take control in Alabama,

Attorney General Nicholas Katzenbach (*Courtesy of AP Images*)

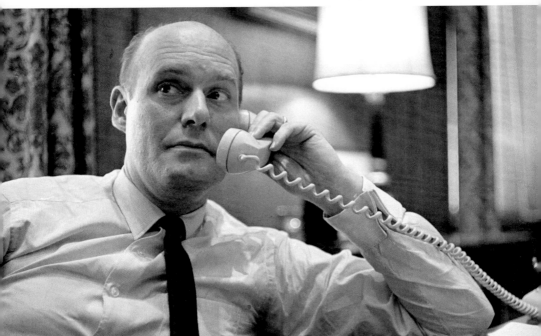

Hosea Williams (right) urges demonstrators in Selma to march to the courthouse. *(Courtesy of AP Images)*

and Katzenbach responded that the FBI was on the case. The SCLC's Hosea Williams was ready to take more direct action. During a speech that day at Selma's Brown Chapel, he urged the congregation to march that very night to the local courthouse. After his talk, Williams was met on the church steps by Public Safety Director Wilson Baker, who said that state troopers and hostile whites would attack night-time marchers in Selma just like they had in Marion. When Williams insisted he would march anyway, he was arrested, and no march was held.

On February 21, the day Malcolm X was assassinated, Selma's African American leaders vowed that the city's black citizens would boycott downtown businesses. The next day, Monday, the focus was on Martin Luther King. In Selma,

King led a march of two hundred elderly African Americans to sign the appearance book at the courthouse, which now had about 2,000 signatures. King also visited Jimmie Lee Jackson in the hospital, spoke at Mount Zion Baptist in Marion, and attended a mass meeting at Brown Chapel. It was a high-profile day for the minister, whose life was in danger. On Monday, the local Citizens' Council (one of the all-white organizations whose goals were to prevent integration) staged a rally in Selma. And that night, Katzenbach personally called King to warn him of an assassination plot against him.

On Tuesday, Alabama governor George Wallace, a hard-line segregationist who had been keeping a low profile during the Selma movement, issued an edict on February 23 banning night marches. Moreover, he sent state troopers to Selma to enforce the new ruling, even though such troopers had acted ruthlessly in Marion. Addressing the same topic, the Alabama Senate proclaimed its support for the troopers, not the protesters, in the Marion debacle. And to further show whose side the state was on, Colonel Al Lingo, head of the Alabama state troopers, served an arrest warrant to Jackson on Tuesday as he lay dying in his hospital bed. The actions on February 23 reflected Wallace's pronouncement when he first became governor in 1963: "Segregation now, segregation tomorrow, segregation forever!"

Protest leaders were ready to speak to Wallace directly. On Tuesday, King told the press that there would be a march on the state capitol building in Montgomery on March 8. Also that day, thirty-one Republicans issued a statement demanding that President Johnson make a move on voting rights. As House Republican Minority Leader (and future

U.S. president) Gerald Ford would say later in the week: "The patience of fair-minded people is wearing thin when, after decades of waiting and three civil rights acts, the basic right of citizenship is still denied to a substantial number of citizens in defiance of the Constitution."

Actually, the Johnson administration and the Justice Department were working on a voting rights bill, one that stressed the elimination of literacy tests and the use of federal registrars. Jimmie Lee Jackson would not see such a law come to fruition. He died at 8:10 a.m. on February 26.

On the afternoon of Jackson's death, the SCLC's James Bevel walked with Selma activist Bernard Lafayette to the home of Jackson's family—a small house in the woods outside of Marion. Cager Lee, Viola Jackson, and Jimmie Lee's sister, Emma, were there, all bruised and bandaged from the February 18 attacks.

James Bevel *(Library of Congress)*

Bevel asked if they would continue marching with the voting rights activists. "Oh, yeah," Lee said. Bevel left their home in tears, contemplating a grandiose march to the state capital.

That evening, Bevel preached at Brown Chapel. Discussing a Bible passage, he told the congregation how Mordecai had

Mourners look on as Jimmie Lee Jackson's casket is carried into a church.
(Courtesy of AP Images)

told Esther to go see the king in order to protect the Jews. Referring to Governor Wallace, Bevel declared, "I must go see the king!" He preached, inspiring the congregation, and announced his plan to march fifty-four miles to the capital. "Be prepared to walk to Montgomery!" he cried. "Be prepared to sleep on the highway!"

Recalled Bevel years later:

> I had to preach, because I had to get the people back out of the state of negative violence and out of a state of grief. If you don't deal with negative violence and grief, it turns into bitterness. So what I recommended was that people walk to Montgomery,

> which would give them time to work through their hostility and resentments and get back to focus on the issue.

Bevel informed the press that the walk to Montgomery would commence on March 7, five days away. The following day, King announced his approval of Bevel's plan. While giving the eulogy at Jackson's funeral at Brown Chapel, King said, "We will bring a voting bill into being on the streets of Selma."

With the march looking like a sure go, local, county, and state officials discussed how to handle the situation. As usual, their motive was to thwart the activists' efforts while not coming across as bullies. To that end, Governor Wallace at first agreed to allow the fifty-four-mile march but to close the roads to vehicles. That way, no one could supply the marchers with food or drink and their march would dwindle to nothing.

However, on Friday, March 5, state representative Bill Edwards from Lowndes County said that if marchers made it to his county, which was sandwiched between Dallas and Montgomery counties, they likely would face shootings and bombings from white supremacists. That day, Wallace along with Colonel Lingo and Major John Cloud of the state troopers agreed that troopers would use nonviolent, nonaggressive means to stop the marchers before they left Selma. Selma Mayor Joseph Smitherman confirmed that the stoppage would be peaceful.

King talked again with President Johnson, this time for seventy-eight minutes. Although they discussed the future voting rights bill and other civil rights issues, King and Johnson did not address the issue of security for the Sunday march. This continued to be a hot subject in Alabama. On Saturday, Wallace changed his strategy completely, announcing that a march on U.S. 80 would be prohibited for the sake of public safety. State troopers, he said, would use any means necessary to prevent the march.

On March 6, several dozen white Alabamans marched to the Selma courthouse in support of the black activists—only to be verbally and physically assaulted by white segregationists.

Also on Saturday, the SNCC leadership debated about whether to participate in the march. SNCC lacked money to support the event, and its members were wary of anticipated police brutality. Moreover, some SNCC leaders were still resentful of the SCLC leaders, whom they felt were grandstanding in Selma and would abandon the city's black citizens once the campaign was over. Eventually, it was agreed that SNCC members could participate in the march but only as individuals, not as representatives of SNCC.

Confusion persisted on march day. At the last minute, Selma City Council members persuaded local police not to join state troopers in halting/assaulting protesters. Meanwhile, King—due to serious concerns about his safety—chose to remain in Atlanta. Earlier, he had told his followers: "I can't promise you that it won't get you beaten. I can't promise you that it won't get your house bombed. I can't promise you won't get scarred up a bit. But we must stand up for what is right!"

On Sunday, March 7, more than six hundred African Americans and a few whites assembled at Brown Chapel on Sylvan Street. The marchers had been briefed about how to best protect themselves from body blows and tear gas. Several ambulances and a small group of doctors and nurses joined the protesters. In King's absence, John Lewis of SNCC and Hosea Williams of the SCLC led the mid-afternoon march.

Lugging bedrolls and knapsacks, the protesters marched along the streets of Selma. They turned onto Broad Street and ascended the Edmund Pettus Bridge, which crossed the Alabama River. This was the pivotal point, since after the bridge ended, U.S. 80 began—and Wallace had prohibited marching on that highway.

As the marchers reached the summit of the bridge, they saw at least fifty state troopers waiting on the far end of the bridge. The troopers were headed by Colonel Lingo, an old friend of Governor Wallace's and a hard-line segregationist. The troopers formed a three-deep line across all four lanes of the highway. Dressed in blue shirts and helmets, they carried billy clubs, guns, and gas masks. Several dozen of Sheriff Clark's posse men waited on the sidelines, some on horseback.

Dozens of local whites watched nearby, while the press was sequestered a hundred yards away near a car dealership. Williams and Lewis feared the worst. Lewis peered over the edge of the bridge, to the muddy water a hundred feet below. "John, can you swim?" Williams asked him. "No, Hosea, I can't swim," Lewis responded. "We're not going back. We're not going to jump. We're going forward."

When the marchers came within a hundred yards of the troopers, a state police officer told the troopers to don their gas masks. Then, after marching another seventy-five yards, the protesters halted. Major John Cloud ordered through a bullhorn: "This is an unlawful assembly. Your march is not conducive to the public safety. You are ordered to disperse and go back to your church or to your homes."

State troopers armed with billy clubs, guns, and gas masks wait for marchers to cross the Edmund Pettus Bridge. *(Library of Congress)*

"May we have a word with the major?" Williams asked. "There is no word to be had," the major replied. Williams asked twice more to speak to Cloud, but was denied each time. Cloud then said, "You have two minutes to turn around and go back to your church." The marchers did not turn around, but Cloud did not give them two minutes, either—only one. At 4:15 p.m., he shouted, "Troopers, advance!"

Troopers rushed toward the protesters. They met the front line of marchers in a violent collision, knocking ten to twenty to the ground, scattering their supply bags in all directions. The troopers pulled out their clubs, batting and wounding the unarmed protestors. From the sidelines, white segregationists cheered the police force, then Clark's deputies and posse men joined the melee.

The protesters tried to retreat, but they stumbled over each other while being pursued from behind. As they ran,

A state trooper rushes into a cloud of tear gas as other troopers beat protesters with their billy clubs. *(Library of Congress)*

canisters were fired into the air. "Tear gas!" cried a marcher. Grayish yellow smoke filled the air. As protesters screamed and coughed and choked, the lawmen intensified their assault. They lashed the African Americans with bull whips; horses of mounted police trampled bodies on the ground. Recounted *Time* magazine:

> "O.K., nigger!" snarled a posseman, flailing away at a running Negro woman. "You wanted to march—now march!"
> "Please! No!" begged a Negro as a cop flailed away with his club.
> "My God, we're being killed!" cried another.

The tear gas stung the eyes of protesters, enveloping them in smoke. "Fifteen or twenty nightsticks could be seen through the gas flailing at the heads of the marchers," wrote *New York Times* reporter Roy Reed.

An officer looks down at a wounded marcher as mounted Dallas County possemen stand by. (*Library of Congress*)

Jim Benston, a protestor, was clubbed on the head. "I was knocked out for maybe five minutes," he said. "When I woke up I was in a cloud. I couldn't breathe and I couldn't see. I was coughing and I was sick. It was like the world had gone away." Benston accused the troopers of using the weight of the horses (approximately one thousand pounds each) to crush the demonstrators. "One posseman tried to get his horse to rear up and land on top of a man near me," Benston said, "but the horse wouldn't do it. Horses have more sense."

Sheyann Webb was among the youngest marchers—just eight years old. She recalled:

> I was blinded by the tears. So I began running and not seeing where I was going. I remember being scared that I might fall over the railing and into the water. I don't know if I was screaming or not, but everyone else was. People were running and falling and

ducking and you could hear the horses' hooves on the pavement and you'd hear people scream and hear the whips swishing and you'd hear them striking the people. They'd cry out; some moaned. Women as well as men were getting hit.

Amelia Boynton, the Dallas County Voters' League leader who Sheriff Clark had shoved down the block on January 19, was hit on the back of the neck by a trooper. When she turned around, he hit her again, knocking her to the ground. John Lewis also was viciously assaulted, suffering a fractured skull.

The marchers retreated manically to town, with the state troopers and deputies and possemen still in pursuit. A few wounded remained on the bridge. They did not receive immediate attention since the police had banned ambulances from the bridge.

SNCC Leader John Lewis holds his head as he is beaten by an Alabama state trooper. *(Courtesy of AP Images)*

Many of the marchers headed back to Brown Chapel, chased and attacked the entire way. Willie Bolden of the SCLC recalled: "They literally whipped folk all the way back to the church. They even came up in the yard of the church, hittin' on folk. Ladies, men, babies, children—they didn't give a damn who they were."

Outside Brown Chapel, some African Americans threw bottles, bricks, and stones at the police, even though such retaliation strictly violated the movement's commitment to nonviolence.

Eventually, Public Safety Director Wilson Baker stepped in. A much more level-headed official than Sheriff Clark, and technically his superior, Baker had been unable to control Clark for weeks. Frustrated and angry with Clark, Baker ordered, "Sheriff, keep your men back." Clark replied: "Everything will be all right. I've already waited a month too damn long!"

Clark did disperse his men, but they continued to harass African Americans in the downtown area. They pounded on the hoods of black citizens' cars and shouted, "Get the hell out of town. We want all niggers off the streets."

Dozens of protesters received emergency treatment at Good Samaritan Hospital. In addition to cuts, bruises, and stinging eyes, victims had suffered fractures of ribs, skulls, arms, and legs. Some estimates put the number of injured as high as one hundred. Sunday March 7 was dubbed "Bloody Sunday."

As protesters, some weeping, huddled into Brown Chapel, John Lewis delivered a speech before going to the hospital. "I don't see how President Johnson can send troops to Vietnam, I don't see how he can send troops to the Congo,

I don't see how he can send troops to Africa and can't send troops to Selma, Alabama," Lewis said. The congregation roared its approval. Though bloody and beaten, the black citizens of Selma were not defeated. They were ready for another march.

A protester carries a child and a sign urging President Johnson to go to Selma. *(Library of Congress)*

four

"We Shall Overcome"

O n Sunday evening, March 7, millions of Americans watched *Judgment at Nuremberg,* a film about the trials of Nazi war criminals. Shortly after 9 p.m. Eastern time, ABC interrupted the movie for a special report. The network aired coverage of the bloody encounter in Selma. TV cameramen had filmed the attack from a distance, but viewers could hear the screams and see the flailing clubs and stampeding horses. George B. Leonard, who watched the report on television recalled:

> A shrill cry of terror, unlike any that had passed through a TV set, rose up as the troopers lumbered forward, stumbling sometimes on the fallen bodies. . . . *Unhuman.* No other word can describe the motions. . . . My wife, sobbing, turned and walked away, saying, "I can't look any more."

The Alabama lawmen were suddenly equated with Hitler and the Nazis. "The violence in Selma was so similar to the violence in Nazi Germany that viewers could hardly miss the connection," wrote the SCLC's Andrew Young. Added Hosea Williams, who had led the march: "I fought in World War II, and I once was captured by the German army, and I want to tell you that the Germans never were as inhuman as the state troopers of Alabama."

While stunned Americans watched the footage on television, several hundred people still remained in Selma's Brown Chapel. Experiencing mixed emotions and unsure of the future of the movement, they were roused by the opening of doors at around 11 p.m. A large group of people, black and white, entered the church. They had heard what had happened and they immediately flew from New Jersey to Alabama on a chartered plane. They said, according to Reverend Frederick Reese, "We are here to share with the people of Selma in this struggle for the vote." The church erupted in spirited applause.

Though stationed in Atlanta, Martin Luther King was plenty busy on Sunday, sending about two hundred telegrams to religious leaders, asking them to join in a repeat march on Tuesday. All over America, leaders of various faiths responded to the call. Episcopal Bishop James Pike and Methodist Bishop John Wesley Lord interrupted their plans and headed for Alabama. So, too, did Catholic Monsignor George L. Gingras and Rabbi Richard G. Hirsch. In all, more than four hundred clergymen would arrive in Selma by Tuesday.

On Monday, the Bloody Sunday attack made bold headlines nationwide. the *New York Times* headline read: "Alabama Police Use Gas and Clubs to Rout Negroes."

On Capitol Hill, congressmen voiced their disgust with the Selma attack and expressed the need for justice. Senator (and

Judge Frank Johnson *(Courtesy of AP Images)*

future Vice President) Walter Mondale (D-MN) called Bloody Sunday an outrage, which required "legislation to guarantee southern Negroes the right to vote an absolute imperative for Congress this year."

On Monday, White House Press Secretary George Reedy told reporters that voting rights legislation was in the works. President Johnson made several calls about Selma and publicly declared that he "deplored the brutality." He also urged both sides in Selma to cool down.

Meanwhile, the Tuesday march that King had proposed was becoming highly problematic. In Montgomery, Alabama, on Monday, two SCLC attorneys met with District Judge Frank Johnson, requesting an injunction against state interference with any future march attempt. Though a supporter of the civil rights movement, Johnson said he would not grant an injunction against state authorities without a hearing, which he scheduled for Thursday.

Judge Johnson advised that until the matter was settled, King should call off the Tuesday march. At 9 o'clock on

Monday evening, the attorneys called the judge to say that King had agreed to postpone.

However, King wasn't sure he had made the right decision. How would he tell the hundreds of clergy, who had journeyed hundreds or even thousands of miles, to go home, that he had made a mistake? Also, King already was being criticized for shying away from the Sunday march. Moreover, many angry African Americans were determined to march again, no matter what some white judge had said.

On the other hand, King wanted to show good faith to Judge Johnson, who had been a friend of the movement. He also didn't want to go against the wishes of his most powerful ally, President Johnson, who opposed a second march. King's hands were further tied when Judge Johnson issued a restraining order that prohibited a march from Selma to Montgomery.

All the way up to the proposed march time on Tuesday, King and others debated about what to do. Attorney General Nicholas Katzenbach offered King a deal: If he would postpone the march, Katzenbach promised that government attorneys would help plead King's case before Judge Johnson on Thursday.

Instead, at 4 a.m. on Tuesday, King and SCLC leaders decided to compromise: The march would go on, but King would end it in Selma before there was any confrontation. That way, he would not violate the Selma to Montgomery restraining order, and he would please the President and protect the marchers by avoiding more violence. Only the SCLC leadership was informed of this plan, although many marchers got wind that the march was going to be short.

Shortly after sunrise, King met with federal Community Relations Service Director LeRoy Collins, who repeated that the President wished that there would be no march at all. By this time, however, King would not be dissuaded. Later in the morning, Sheriff Clark and Colonel Lingo told Collins that they would not allow the marchers to proceed toward Montgomery. Collins asked if violence would be avoided if the marchers turned around and retreated after they reached the troopers' line. They said yes. Collins relayed this information to King.

Just prior to the march, with plans now in place, King spoke: "I have made my choice. I have got to march. I do not know what lies ahead of us. There may be beatings, jailings, tear gas. But I would rather die on the highways of Alabama than make a butchery of my conscience!"

Around 2:30 p.m., King led approximately 2,000 citizens (including the four hundred clergy members) on their march to the Edmund Pettus Bridge. When they reached the foot of the bridge, U.S. Marshal H. Stanley Fountain read to them

Protesters march over the bridge and toward the city limits of Selma and waiting state troopers. *(Courtesy of AP Images)*

U.S. Marshal H. Stanley Fountain reads Judge Johnson's restraining order to King and the marchers. *(Library of Congress)*

Judge Johnson's restraining order. King informed the marshal that they were proceeding anyway.

The protesters cleared the bridge and walked a couple hundred more yards before reaching the line of lawmen. Major John Cloud, through his bullhorn, ordered the marchers to halt. King asked if some of the religious leaders could recite several prayers. The protesters first sang "We Shall Overcome," then prayers were said by four different clergymen. As hundreds knelt, Reverend Ralph Abernathy of the SCLC prayed: "We come to present our bodies as a living sacrifice. We don't have much to offer, but we do have our bodies, and we lay them on the altar today."

After the prayers, King turned around and proceeded to lead his followers back across the bridge. Assistant Attorney General John Doar, who was on the scene, informed Katzenbach in

Washington of the turnaround. Katzenbach in turn informed the White House that violence had been avoided. President Johnson, who had been under criticism for not protecting citizens in Alabama, was undoubtedly relieved.

The marchers wondered what was going on, and they were further confused when the troopers moved to the sides of the road as if to let the group proceed toward Montgomery. This unexpected move apparently was meant to embarrass King, to give the illusion that he was afraid and betraying his people. But the clearance came only after King's retreat, and it would become obvious later that this was just game-playing on the part of Alabama officials.

Nevertheless, as they turned around and headed back over the bridge, most marchers felt disappointed with King, as well as frustrated and angry. Reverend Orloff Miller recalled marching "back over the bridge with a terrible sinking feeling. It felt just awful. I had come to lay myself on the line just as much as people in Selma had done only forty-eight hours before. And here I was in a turnaround march."

When they returned to the church, King tried to assuage hurt feelings. "At least we had to get to the point where the brutality took place," he told the gathering. "And we made it clear when we got there that we were going to have some form of protest and worship. I can assure you that something happened in Alabama that's never happened before. When Negroes and whites can stand on Highway 80 and have a mass meeting, things aren't that bad."

King's words fell short of a full explanation and did not satisfy everyone. SNCC members, long resentful of King and the SCLC, felt especially betrayed. After

King speaks to a crowd of protesters after they return from the aborted march. *(Library of Congress)*

"Turnaround Tuesday," as the day was subsequently called, SNCC leaders decided to focus their efforts on Montgomery instead of Selma.

Despite two aborted marches in three days, the voting rights campaign, on a national level, was proceeding at great speed. On Tuesday, outraged citizens in numerous cities staged demonstrations in support of civil rights. In Detroit, Mayor Jerome Cavanaugh and Michigan governor George Romney, both white, led a protest parade of 10,000 people. Another thousand marched in Washington, D.C.

On the floors of the Senate and House of Representatives on Tuesday, no fewer than fifty congressmen condemned Sunday's debacle and called for voting rights legislation. One Democratic senator said that unless the Johnson administration acted quickly, "northern Democratic liberals will put in a bill of their own."

On Tuesday, approximately six hundred demonstrators gathered at the White House to protest what they alleged was inaction on the part of the president. In truth, Johnson was already moving forward with a voting rights bill. And with the Congress and the nation appalled by Bloody Sunday, he wanted to strike while the fire was hot.

On Tuesday afternoon, President Johnson issued a written statement to the press via George Reedy:

> Ever since the events of Sunday afternoon in Selma, Alabama, the Administration has been in close touch with the situation and has made every effort to prevent a repetition. I am certain Americans everywhere join me in deploring the brutality with which a number of Negro citizens of Alabama were treated when they sought to dramatize their deep and sincere interest in attaining the precious right to vote.

Johnson stated that the "best legal talent in the federal government is engaged in preparing legislation which will secure that right for every American." He added that a federal district court in Alabama had been requested to enjoin state officials from interfering with a Selma to Montgomery march. And he urged leaders "to approach this tense situation with calmness, reasonableness, and respect for the law."

Reverend James Reeb was a Unitarian-Universalist minister who worked primarily with impoverished African Americans in Boston. He was an ardent supporter of civil rights, and for the Tuesday march, Reeb had traveled to Selma, one of the four hundred clergy men invited by King. After the march, Reeb and two other Unitarian clergymen ate dinner at a black diner in Selma. Afterward, they walked past the Silver Moon Cafe, a hangout popular among white segregationists.

Mayor Smitherman (left) and Public Safety Director Wilson Baker speak
to the press as they prepare to block a march to the Selma courthouse.
(Courtesy of AP Images)

As the clergymen walked past the cafe, they were attacked.
Reeb was struck on the skull. The ministers escaped, but Reeb
was disoriented and in need of medical attention. Several hours
later, he arrived at Birmingham's University Hospital.

The next day was a busy one in Alabama. Reeb hovered
near death in the Birmingham hospital. In Montgomery, the
SNCC led a demonstration of seven hundred college students. And in Selma, Reverend Abernathy led a march to
the courthouse, which was blocked by Mayor Smitherman
and Public Safety Director Wilson Baker. In Washington,
D.C., a dozen congressmen issued statements about Selma
and voting rights.

On Thursday, March 11, the issue was near the top of
President Johnson's agenda (along with the ever-escalat-
ing war in Vietnam). At one point during the day, Johnson

learned that twelve people were staging a civil rights sit-in in the White House. After debating about how to handle the situation, Johnson had them quietly removed, making sure there was no press coverage. The president also addressed a gathering of sixty congressmen, with whom he discussed Selma and what should be included in the voting rights bill.

In Montgomery on Thursday, Judge Johnson—as promised—began hearings about whether protesters could march from Selma to Montgomery without hindrance. But the biggest story of the day occurred in Birmingham. Reverend Reeb, father of four children, was pronounced dead. He was the second casualty of Selma, after Jimmie Lee Jackson, and significantly, the first white person to die for the cause.

The White House reacted quickly to Reeb's death. The president sent flowers as well as a jet plane to return Reeb's wife and her father-in-law to Boston. First Lady Ladybird Johnson and Vice President Humphrey spoke to Reeb's wife on the phone. Within two days, local police arrested four men for the assault and murder: William Hoggle, his brother O'Neal, R. B. Kelly, and Elmer Cook. Cook, age forty-one, had been arrested twenty-five times, including seventeen on assault charges.

The Reeb murder infuriated millions. Throughout the country, civil rights groups staged protest demonstrations. The AFL-CIO, the American Jewish Committee, and the United Steelworkers Union all officially voiced their outrage. North Dakota Governor William Guy sent Wallace a telegram criticizing the white supremacist attitude of Alabama. Pianist Byron Janis protested by canceling a concert in Mobile. In Selma, a large group of black citizens, white clergymen, and

King carries a wreath as he and others make their way toward a memorial service for Unitarian minister Rev. James Reeb. From left to right (front) His Eminence Iakobos, Archbishop of the Greek Orthodox Church, King, Revs. Ralph Abernathy and Andrew Young. *(Courtesy of AP Images)*

white Catholic nuns held a peaceful vigil that lasted deep into the night.

Even a white southern politician spoke out about the violence in Alabama. "I abhor this brutality," stated Texas Democratic Senator Ralph Yarborough. "Shame on you, George Wallace, for the wet ropes that bruised the muscles, for the bull whips that cut the flesh, for the clubs that broke the bones, for the tear gas that blinded, burned, and choked into insensibility!"

The sudden flurry of activity surprised many African Americans. After all, the murder of Jimmie Lee Jackson had riled the local black community but had caused hardly a stir among the nation's whites. Why was America so much more upset over Reeb's passing? Indeed, Jackson's death had been even more appalling—shot twice after trying to save his mother and grandfather, then beaten some more, all by or under the eye of state officials.

Stokely Carmichael, an emerging young leader of SNCC, recognized that even outside the South, a white person's life still was deemed more valuable than a black person's. "What you want," he said, "is the nation to be upset when anybody is killed . . . but it almost [seems that] for this to be recognized, a white person must be killed."

The president devoted most of his workday on Friday to the Selma situation. In a pair of two-hour meetings, he talked with various religious leaders, who voiced their displeasure with Johnson's lack of action in Selma—especially his reluctance to send federal troops. Later in the afternoon, Johnson held a meeting with top brass to discuss voting rights legislation and the Selma situation. The president made arrangements to meet with Governor Wallace, who agreed to fly in on Saturday morning.

When George Wallace flew to Washington on Saturday, March 13, demonstrations still raged in the nation's capital

Alabama governor George Wallace *(Courtesy of AP Images)*

and other major cities. Just before noon, Wallace and his aides met with President Johnson, Attorney General Katzenbach, and others. From there, Johnson took Wallace to the Oval Office for a private meeting.

Johnson had no patience for Wallace's brand of racism. A large, domineering man, who like Wallace hailed from the South, Johnson later wrote that he stared directly into his guest's eyes the whole time, and that the governor appeared nervous and aggressive. Predictably, Wallace defended his law-enforcement policies while blaming the demonstrators for all the recent problems.

Recalled U.S. Justice Department staff member Burke Marshall, who was at the larger meeting:

> In the meeting, the President totally snowed him. Governor Wallace didn't quite grovel, but he was so pliant by the end of the two hours, with President Johnson putting his arm around him, and telling him it's a moment of history. And how do we want to be remembered, as petty little men, or do we want to be remembered as great figures that faced up to our moments of crisis?

After the meeting, both Wallace and Johnson met with the press. Johnson, who anticipated that the federal court would lift the ban on the march, hoped that the governor would tell the press that he would protect the marchers in Alabama. Instead, Wallace's comments were ambiguous.

Johnson, though, did not mince words. "What happened in Selma was an American tragedy," he said. "It is wrong to do violence to peaceful citizens in the streets of their town. It is wrong to deny Americans the right to vote. It is wrong to deny any person full equality because of the color of his skin."

President Johnson ended the address by listing three steps that he had advised Governor Wallace to take: publicly declare his support for universal suffrage; assure peaceful assemblies in Alabama; and hold biracial meetings in order to achieve interracial cooperation. Covering all bases, the President declared that federal troops were ready to protect marchers in Selma if needed. He added that he hoped that the administration's voting rights bill would be sent to Congress by Monday.

Selma and voting rights dominated the weekend papers, even receiving substantial international coverage. How could America trumpet democracy worldwide, the foreign press asked, when it denied it to its own people? Such a topic was especially sensitive in 1965 as the president needed to justify his escalating war in Vietnam, which was ostensibly about preventing the spread of communism and preserving democracy in South Vietnam.

Politically aware African Americans also saw the hypocrisy: Why should they risk their lives fighting for the South Vietnamese people's freedoms when they themselves weren't even able to vote? Later in the war, Stokely Carmichael would hand out satirical flyers that said "Fight for Freedom . . . (in Viet Nam)" and "Receive valuable training in the skills of killing off other oppressed people!"

President Johnson also understood the hypocrisy, and other nations' criticism of such, which likely contributed to his desire to end all civil rights injustices as soon as possible. George Wallace, meanwhile, continued to be a roadblock. On Sunday, March 14, Wallace appeared on the CBS show *Face the Nation*. He criticized the recent press coverage of Alabama, calling it excessive and distorted. But on

Sunday, the American people proved that it wasn't just the media who cared about the events in Alabama. At Lafayette Park in Washington, D.C., the National Council of Churches sponsored a demonstration attended by 15,000 people. And in Boston, 20,000 showed up for a memorial service for James Reeb.

At 5 p.m. on Sunday, the president held a large meeting with Vice President Humphrey, Attorney General Katzenbach, and more than a dozen senior members of Congress. After an hour and a half of discussion, they agreed that on Monday evening Johnson would address a joint session of Congress—an event typically staged for topics of the utmost importance—to promote the voting rights bill that he was about to submit. The address would be televised by all three major networks.

Throughout Sunday evening, Johnson and staff members discussed the wording of the address, which speechwriter Richard Goodwin would write overnight. During the evening, the president personally called Martin Luther King, NAACP Executive Director Roy Wilkins, and National Urban League Executive Director Whitney Young to invite them to Monday's address.

Monday, March 15, turned out to be one of the great breakthrough days in the history of the civil rights movement. In Alabama, Lowndes and Wilcox counties registered black voters for the first time ever. In Selma, 2,000 protesters gathered for a memorial for James Reeb. Led by King, the service was attended by congressmen, bishops, and even United Auto Workers President Walter P. Reuther. Wilson Baker kept the peace while Sheriff Clark and his men stewed on the sidelines.

Throughout Monday, President Johnson worked on the final details of his speech. At about 9 pm, he addressed the nation's senators and representatives as well as 70 million viewers. King watched on television in Alabama.

After expounding on the meaning of democracy, the President got to the central issue. "Every American citizen must have an equal right to vote," he stated.

> There is no reason which can excuse the denial of that right. . . . Yet the harsh fact is that in many places in this country, men and women are kept from voting simply because they are Negroes. . . . Every device of which human ingenuity is capable has been used to deny this right. The Negro citizen may go to register only to be told that the day is wrong, or the hour is late, or the official in charge is absent. And if he persists and, if he manages to present himself to the registrar, he may be disqualified because he did not spell out his middle name, or because he abbreviated a word on the application. And if he manages to fill out an application, he is given a test. The registrar is the sole judge of whether he passes this test. He may be asked to recite the entire Constitution, or explain the most complex provisions of state law. And even a college degree cannot be used to prove that he can read and write. For the fact is that the only way to pass these barriers is to show a white skin.

Next, Johnson discussed the details of the bill he was about to submit to Congress. He said the bill would outlaw all restrictions that had been used to deny African Americans the right to vote. It would allow federal workers to register voters if local registrars refused to do so. It would eliminate tedious, unnecessary lawsuits that delayed the right to vote, and it would ensure that properly registered citizens would not be prohibited from voting on Election Day.

Johnson implored southern registrars:

> Open your polling places to all your people. Allow men and women to register and vote whatever the color of their skin. Extend the rights of citizenship to every citizen of this land. . . . We ought not, and we cannot, and we must not wait another eight months before we get a bill. We have already waited a hundred years and more, and the time for waiting is gone. So I ask you to join me in working long hours and nights and weekends, if necessary, to pass this bill.

About halfway through the address, the president delivered what would become the most oft-quoted lines of the speech: "It is the effort of American Negroes to secure for themselves the full blessings of American life. Their cause must be our cause, too. Because it's not just Negroes, but really it's all of us, who must overcome the crippling legacy of bigotry and injustice. And we *shall* overcome."

With those last three words, Johnson had taken the anthem of the civil rights movement and made it the mission statement of America. The words earned a thunderous round of applause, one of many that interrupted the forty-five minute speech. Twice the president received a standing ovation.

C. T. Vivian of the SCLC recalled watching the address on television with Martin Luther King:

> When we heard [President Johnson] give that famous speech, we were all sitting around together. Martin was sitting in a chair looking toward the TV set, and when LBJ said, "And we shall overcome," we all cheered. I looked over toward Martin and Martin was very quietly sitting in the chair, and a tear ran down his cheek. It was a victory like none other, it was an affirmation of the movement, it guaranteed us as much as anything that we

would vote and that millions of people in the South would have a chance to be involved in their own destiny.

The following morning, Tuesday, March 16, many Americans awoke with a new sense of purpose. On Capitol Hill, congressmen lauded the speech and predicted a quick passage of the voting rights bill. Supreme Court Justice William O. Douglas was among the many who personally praised the President for his speech, writing in a note: "absolutely superb . . . the best ever."

On Tuesday, six hundred people, largely white students from the North, protested outside the state capitol in Montgomery. This deeply angered segregationists, who despised what they called "outside agitators." On horseback

A college student calls for help to aid a fellow demonstrator while, in the background, an injured girl is carried away after segregationists attacked civil rights workers in Montgomery, Alabama. *(Courtesy of AP Images/Perry Aycock)*

and on foot, segregationist lawmen attacked the protesters with billy clubs and cattle prods. Eight people were injured. Yet the attack would be the last cathartic release for white supremacists, at least during this campaign. Later that day, one thousand demonstrators marched in Montgomery, this time under police protection.

Good news arrived on Wednesday. Federal Judge Frank Johnson ruled that demonstrators were allowed to march from Selma to Montgomery, and that local and state officials could not impede their march. He stated: "The law is clear that the right to petition one's government for the redress of grievances may be exercised in large groups . . . and these rights may be exercised by marching, even along public highways."

Johnson went on to approve a Selma to Montgomery march plan submitted by SCLC attorneys. The judge ruled that unlimited marching on U.S. 80 was acceptable when the highway widened to four lanes. When it was two lanes, three hundred people at a time could walk. Johnson also said that the Justice Department had offered to provide troops to protect the marchers if needed. Late on Wednesday, the SCLC's Hosea Williams informed the press that a Selma to Montgomery march would commence on March 21, exactly two weeks after Bloody Sunday.

Several thousand men protected the marchers, including approximately 1,000 military police, 1,900 federalized Alabama national guardsmen, and assorted U.S. marshals and FBI personnel. Troops bearing rifles stood at every crossroad, and soldiers checked for bombs and mines at scheduled sleeping areas.

Once U.S. 80 dwindled from four lanes to two, only three hundred people were allowed to continue the march. Thus, most people went home on Sunday. Rev. Ralph Abernathy was one of the three hundred who continued the journey.

Abernathy recalled:

> The final march was enjoyable and it was tension-filled all at the same time. We had to march on one side of the highway, and the cars had to move on the other side. A great deal of profanity was yelled from the passing cars, and the old farmers came out, mostly white people, and they looked at us with utter disdain. But we knew that the victory was in sight.

A national guardsman stands on duty during the first day of the march as civil rights activists head for Montgomery. *(Courtesy of AP Images)*

On Sunday, marchers walked seven of the scheduled fifty-four miles before retiring at a campsite, where volunteers provided gear and food. SCLC official Andrew Young explained the logistics of the march:

> The March from Selma to Montgomery was, from my perspective, a job. We had three hundred people to feed every day. We had to find a place to pitch tents, and we had to be concerned about security all along the road. There was absolutely nothing romantic about it. I was running back and forth, mostly with Ivanhoe Donaldson of SNCC, trying to keep the march together and solving problems from one end to the other. I figure anytime they marched ten miles, I did closer to forty.

Monday through Wednesday were the most grueling days. Still walking along the two-lane road, the marchers logged sixteen miles on Monday, eleven on Tuesday, and sixteen on Wednesday. It was a long haul, but black Southerners were used to a hard life. It rained on Monday, turning the evening's campsite into a muddy mess, but nicer weather returned.

Throughout the journey, marchers sang "freedom songs." "I will never forget a little song that one of the guys would sing—'Pick 'em up, put 'em down'—all the way from Selma," remembered John Lewis. The SNCC leader felt the march "was like a holy crusade, like Gandhi's march to the sea. You didn't get tired, you really didn't get weary, you had to go. It was no ordinary march. To me there was never a march like this one before, and there hasn't been one since."

"The teenagers were a great inspiration," added Amelia Boynton. "I was much impressed with a fifteen-year-old Selma

The marchers rest as they near the midway point of their march to Montgomery. *(Library of Congress)*

boy, [Leroy] Moton. His face beamed with pride as he carried the American flag. . . . Every now and then he would burst into song and we would we join him, often singing 'The Star-Spangled Banner.'"

Sheyann Webb, an eight-year-old girl who had experienced the savagery of Bloody Sunday, also partook in this march. In her book *Selma, Lord, Selma,* she recalled her and friend Rachel's encounter with Martin Luther King. After marching to the freedom song "Ain't Gonna Let Nobody Turn Me 'Round," they caught the attention of the civil rights leader:

"Aren't you tired?" he says.

And me and Rachel shrugged and grinned, and I said, "My feet and legs be tired, but my soul still feels like marchin'."

So he said that we had walked far enough for little girls and he wanted us to get on the bus and go back to Selma. So we said we'd do that and he touched us on the head and went on down the road. I remember standing there a long time and watching those people marching along. I would never forget that sight.

And I said to Rachel, "It seem like we marchin' to Heaven today."

And she says, "Ain't we?"

Though the march was pervaded with a sense of triumph, racist whites did what they could to ruin the event. There was the typical heckling and cold stares, and a small plane dropped leaflets threatening to cut off jobs to those blacks who marched. "An unemployed agitator ceases to agitate," the leaflets said. Later, the 141-member Alabama state legislature would unanimously pass a resolution stating that there had been "evidence of much fornication" at the marchers' camp-sites and that "young women are returning to their respective states apparently as unwed expectant mothers."

Another plot to assassinate Martin Luther King was uncovered. Andrew Young, however, thought up an idea to foil potential snipers. King always wore a "preacher's blue suit." So Young decided to place a group of black preachers about King's height in blue suits and on the front line with King. Hopefully, Young thought, the plan would confuse any potential sniper. "We just had to kind of believe that it was true when white folks said we all look alike," Young said.

On Wednesday, March 24, as the marchers approached Montgomery, U.S. 80 widened to four lanes. Thus, the three-hundred limit was off, and thousands joined in for the remaining few miles to the state capital. Approximately 2,000 demonstrators made camp that night in the City of Jude, thirty-six acres outside Montgomery that were owned by the Catholic Church.

More than 25,000 people gather near the State House in Montgomery to demand equal voting rights. *(Library of Congress)*

That night, big-name entertainers performed for the marchers. African Americans Harry Belafonte, Nipsey Russell, and Sammy Davis Jr. delighted the gatherings, as did white entertainers such as Shelley Winters and Joan Baez.

On Thursday morning, March 25, the protesters marched from City of Jude to their final destination, the State House on Union Street in Montgomery. More than 25,000 people, waving American flags and cheering and singing, gathered for a rally. All three major television networks broadcast the event live. State troopers and other officers guarded the State House, where Governor George Wallace watched the proceedings through Venetian blinds and binoculars.

After two hours of speeches about civil rights and freedom, Martin Luther King, the man many had come to see, rose to address the crowd. "There never was a moment in American history," he said, "more honorable and more inspiring than the pilgrimage of clergymen and laymen of every race and faith pouring into Selma to face danger at the side of its embattled Negroes."

King implored the masses to ride the momentum, to carry through with their fight for voting rights:

> Let us march on ballot boxes until race-baiters disappear from the political arena. Let us march on ballot boxes until the salient misdeeds of bloodthirsty mobs will be transformed into the calculated good deeds of orderly citizens. Let us march on ballot boxes until the Wallaces of our nation tremble away in silence.

King ended his 3,300-word speech with the lyrics of "The Battle Hymn of the Republic," and walked away amid thundering applause. The rally concluded with an attempt by twenty black Alabamans to deliver a petition for voting rights to Governor Wallace. Not unexpectedly, they were turned away by a staff member. After the speech, Wallace went on television to denounce the march, calling it a "prostitution of lawful process."

Though it was a triumphant day, those in attendance could not stick around to savor the moment. The SCLC emphasized to the rally-goers that they leave the area as soon as possible to avoid possible attacks by racist whites.

Some people volunteered to provide transportation, including Viola Liuzzo of Detroit. A white mother of five, Liuzzo drove activists to Selma after the rally and then, in the evening, drove back to Montgomery with black activist Leroy Moton. At 8:00 p.m., a carload of Ku Klux Klansman pulled up next to Liuzzo's car, and shot her dead. Moton feigned death, avoiding a fatal bullet.

Several hours later, FBI agent Gary Thomas Rowe informed his office that he was one of the four Klansmen who had shot Liuzzo and Moton. Early Sunday morning,

Civil rights workers, surrounded by members of the press, conduct a memorial service at the site of Viola Liuzzo's murder. *(Courtesy of AP Images)*

Rowe and the other three men were taken into custody. On Friday, a furious President Johnson addressed the nation to announce the arrests and condemn the Ku Klux Klan.

> [Viola Liuzzo] was murdered by the enemies of justice who for decades have used the rope and the gun and the tar and the feathers to terrorize their neighbors. They struck by night, as they generally do, for their purpose cannot stand the light of day. . . . If Klansmen hear my voice today, let it be both an appeal—and a warning—to get out of the Ku Klux Klan now and return to a decent society—before it is too late.

The Liuzzo murder dominated headlines that weekend, shattering the notion that black Americans had "overcome." Jim Crow was still alive and kicking. He was well armed, and he still wielded nearly all the political power in the South. Only with a new voting rights bill, still under review in Congress in spring 1965, would southern blacks have the weapon to bring Jim Crow to his knees.

six

Breakthrough at the Ballot Box

I
n the Selma to Montgomery march, citizens from across the nation had sent a loud, clear message to Congress: Pass a law that would guarantee voting rights to all Americans. Before and after the March 25 Montgomery rally, debates continued on Capitol Hill about the bill. A few southern congressmen objected to the whole idea of new legislation, but most senators and representatives supported the bill. Some were troubled by certain provisions, and for the next four months, congressmen debated the specifics of the voting rights bill.

Meanwhile, civil rights leaders kept up the pressure. On Saturday, March 27, the SCLC's James Orange led hundreds of marchers to the courthouse in Selma. The next day on *Meet the Press,* Martin Luther King called for a nationwide boycott of Alabama products. That idea was widely criticized, including by the president, as it would hurt black Alabama workers as well as whites.

As the weeks wore on, it appeared that the Selma campaign—as SNCC workers had feared—had done little to help local black citizens. Despite the efforts of thousands who had attempted to vote at the courthouse, black registration in Dallas County had increased from about to 250 to just six hundred by April. The backlash was even worse than the progress, as an estimated 150 African Americans who worked for local whites lost their jobs. Weekly meetings, regarding improving conditions for Selma's black residents, were held between local black leaders and Mayor Joseph Smitherman, but virtually no progress was made.

Perseverance, however, paid off. Through the spring and summer, SCLC staffer Harold Middlebrook pushed forward with voting registration efforts. By mid-July, the number of registered voters in Dallas County rose to nearly 1,500 (although registrars did turn down about half of all black applicants).

Still, the greatest results from the Selma campaign were not local but national. In August 3, 1965, the U.S. House of Representatives passed the Voting Rights Act of 1965 by a resounding vote of 328 to 74 (82 percent in favor). The next day, senators approved it 79 to 18 (81 percent).

Despite months of congressional wrangling, the essence of the Voting Rights Act was relatively simple. The new law banned biased literacy and government tests and other exclusionary screening devices used by registrars to keep African Americans from registering. The act also allowed federal workers to register black voters in areas that had less than 50 percent of eligible black voters registered.

On Friday, August 6, President Johnson signed the act into law in a televised ceremony at the U.S. Capitol. SNCC leader

John Lewis stood near the president, who gave him one of the pens he used. ("I cherish that pen today," Lewis said.)

In a speech after the ceremony, Johnson began by saying, "Today is a triumph for freedom as huge as any victory that has ever been won on any battlefield." The President then summarized events leading up to the historic moment, from slavery to Selma. He continued:

> There were those who said smaller and more gradual measures should be tried. But they had been tried. For years and years they had been tried, and tried, and tried, and they had failed, and failed, and failed. And the time for failure is gone. . . . This law covers many pages. But the heart of the act is plain. Wherever, by clear and objective standards, states and counties are using regulations, or laws, or tests to deny the right to vote, then they will be struck down. If it is clear that state officials still intend to discriminate, then federal examiners will be sent in to register all eligible voters. When the prospect of discrimination is gone, the examiners will be immediately withdrawn.

President Johnson signs the Voting Rights Act of 1965. *(Courtesy of AP Images)*

Johnson addressed African Americans directly:

> Let me now say to every Negro in this country: You must
> register. You must vote. You must learn, so your choice advances
> your interest and the interest of our beloved nation. Your future,
> and your children's future, depend upon it, and I don't believe
> that you are going to let them down.

Unlike the civil rights acts of 1957, 1960, and 1964,
the 1965 act would prove profoundly effective in battling
voting injustice. In fact, on the very day after Johnson
signed the act into law, the U.S. Justice Department filed
suit against the use of the poll tax in Mississippi. Also on
August 7, Attorney General Nicholas Katzenbach's office
began notifying officials in the deep South that all "tests and
devices" related to voter registration were invalid.

On August 10, examiners with the Civil Service
Commission (CSC) began registering black citizens to vote
in nine southern counties. By day's end, the examiners had

Three women process voter registration applications from several hundred
African Americans in Americus, Georgia, shortly after the passage of the
Voting Rights Act of 1965. *(Courtesy of AP Images/Dozier Mobley)*

Selma resident Annie Maude Williams displays her voter registration card after successfully registering to vote. *(Courtesy of AP Images/Dozier Mobley)*

listed more than 1,100 applicants, including more than one hundred in Dallas County. The CSC sent more examiners to more counties, and by the end of August they had officially processed 27,463 black registrants. By late October, the number had risen to 56,000.

In addition, according to the Justice Department, local officials in Alabama, Mississippi, Georgia, and Louisiana registered approximately 32,000 black applicants from August 6 through the end of the month. By late October, that number had soared to 110,000. Registration numbers continued to rise rapidly into 1966.

More good news arrived on March 7, 1966, when the U.S. Supreme Court affirmed the constitutionality of the Voting Rights Act. Later in the month, the high court ruled that poll taxes were unconstitutional.

By the time of the Alabama elections in May 1966, black registrants in that state had quickly doubled to 235,000, representing a quarter of Alabama's total registered voters. For the first time, candidates began to appeal to black citizens for their vote. In a campaign for Jefferson County sheriff, Al Lingo—one of the men who had orchestrated the Bloody Sunday attacks—intentionally had himself photographed contributing money to the SCLC. And incredibly enough, Dallas County Sheriff Jim Clark hosted a barbeque for black voters in his bid to win reelection. He was ousted in favor of Wilson Baker in the 1966 election.

From 1966 forward, white candidates realized that they would lose the black vote, and the election, if they adhered to the old segregationist platform. They would need to be more moderate and take blacks' needs into consideration. In fact, in November 1966, black voters helped moderate white candidates win the governorships of Arkansas and South Carolina. Also that November, African American Lucius Amerson won the race for sheriff in Macon County, Alabama—a victory that would not have been possible without the Voting Rights Act.

From 1964 to 1966, the estimated number of registered black voters in Alabama rose from 111,000 (23 percent of the black population) to 246,000 (51 percent). In Mississippi, the percentage of registered black voters soared from 6.7 percent in 1964 to 33 percent in 1966 to 59 percent in 1968. It should be noted that white voter registration also rose in the South during that period, as campaign workers tried extra hard to keep white politicians in power.

In the late 1960s and beyond, some whites continued to bend the law. Legislatures tried to make certain positions appointive rather than elective so that an African American couldn't be voted in. Whites in some areas made polling

Carl Stokes is sworn in as mayor of Cleveland in 1967, becoming the first elected black mayor of a major U.S. city. *(Courtesy of AP Images)*

places hard to get to in black neighborhoods; others made it difficult for black candidates to get on the ballot.

Despite such efforts, more and more black candidates won elections. By the end of 1970, 711 African Americans held elected positions in the eleven southern states—nearly ten times more than in 1965. In 1969, Charles Evers, brother of civil rights martyr Medgar Evers, made history by becoming the first black mayor of a racially mixed Mississippi town since Reconstruction.

In the late 1960s and the 1970s, African Americans gained more and more political clout. In 1967, high voter

In 1983, Jesse Jackson became the first African American to make a strong bid for the U.S. presidency. *(Library of Congress)*

turnout by black Americans helped Carl Stokes (Cleveland) and Richard Hatcher (Gary, Indiana) become the first black mayors of major U.S. cities. In 1973, Tom Bradley became mayor of Los Angeles, the second most-populous city in the United States. Maynard Jackson was elected mayor of the South's biggest city, Atlanta, in 1973, and Richard Arrington Jr. became mayor of the South's most notoriously racist city, Birmingham, in 1979.

African American Edward Brooke (R-MA) served in the Senate from 1967 to '79, and in 1992, Carol Moseley-Braun (D-IL) became the first black woman to be elected to the U.S. Senate. In 1989, Douglas Wilder of Virginia became the first black governor of the 20th century. And in 1984 and 1988, Democrat Jesse Jackson became the first African American to make a strong bid for the U.S. presidency. Jackson, a disciple of Martin Luther King, was even the front-runner among Democrats for a while in 1988.

Although he did not win the '88 nomination, Jackson inspired millions of minorities with his message of hope—a hope made possible by laws that guaranteed freedom for all. "I was born in the slum, but the slum was not born in me," Jackson said at the 1988 Democratic National Convention. "And it wasn't born in you, and you can make it. Hold your head high, stick your chest out. You can make it. It gets dark sometimes, but the morning comes. Don't you surrender."

seven

Life After Selma

Many activists claimed the Selma campaign to be a triumphant final battle in the successful fight for civil rights. The 1954 *Brown v. Board of Education* ruling had outlawed segregation in schools; the Montgomery bus boycott, the sit-in movement, and the 1964 Civil Rights Act had led to desegregated public facilities; and the 1965 Voting Rights Act secured the right to vote for all black citizens. Legally, the civil rights war had been won.

In reality, however, African Americans had a long way to go to achieve true equality. In southern states in the late 1960s, many school districts continued to resist desegregation. With poor education, little money, and the persistence of racist attitudes, southern blacks found it almost impossible to achieve the "American Dream."

Life was not much better for blacks in northern cities, including Chicago, Detroit, Cleveland, and others. Generally unwelcome in the suburbs and in the "nice" parts of the cities, millions of African Americans remained in the ghettos. There, public facilities and schools received far less funding than in the more affluent suburbs. Moreover, large highway systems that dissected cities tended to "wall off" black residents within their neighborhoods. Few businesses were willing to invest in such areas.

Recognizing the troubles up north, Martin Luther King launched a campaign against housing discrimination in Chicago in 1966. It was far from successful. On August 5, King led a march in the Marquette Park neighborhood of Chicago, where whites were adamant about preventing blacks from moving in. Large throngs of whites disrupted the demonstration with signs ("The Only Way to End Niggers Is Exterminate"), bottles, firecrackers, and rocks—one of which hit King in the head. King said he had never experienced such hatred, not even in the Ku Klux Klan strongholds of the deep South.

In the mid-to late 1960s, many African Americans rejected King's doctrine of nonviolent protest. Although the SCLC remained true to the cause, SNCC turned more and more militant. These activists were, as Fanny Lou Hamer famously said, "sick and tired of being sick and tired."

As young blacks became more culturally aware during the civil rights movement, many seethed with anger over what they saw: centuries of black oppression, much of which remained in the form of economic subjugation and police brutality. Moreover, because young men not in college were more likely to be drafted, a disproportionate number of black men were sent to Vietnam, where thousands died.

On June 16, 1966, young SNCC radical Stokely Carmichael unofficially launched the Black Power movement. "The only way we gonna stop them white men from whuppin' us is to take over," Carmichael preached during a rally in Greenwood, Mississippi. "We been saying 'freedom' for six years and we ain't got nothin'! What we gonna start saying now is 'Black Power!'"

In the fall of 1966, Bobby Seale and Huey Newton formed the militant Black Panther Party. Some of their goals were perceived as justified, such as full employment, decent housing, and quality medical care for all black Americans. However, at times, they advocated violence and revolution to achieve their aims. SNCC Chairman H. Rap Brown spoke for many young blacks in 1967 when he declared, "If America don't come around, we're going to burn it down!"

Militant rhetoric, pervasive black anger, and subsequent crackdowns by white police officers fueled feelings of desperation, and America's ghettos became tinderboxes ready to explode. Beginning in the Watts section of Los Angeles in August 1965, riots erupted in major cities across the nation. Thirty-four people died

H. Rap Brown *(Library of Congress)*

in the Watts riot; forty-three lay dead in Detroit in July 1967; and twenty-five were killed in Newark, New Jersey, that same month.

On April 4, 1968, white Southerner James Earl Ray assassinated Martin Luther King in Memphis, Tennessee. In the aftermath, hatred between blacks and whites raged across America. Violence and destruction tore apart more than 120 communities, with forty-six people killed. In Washington, D.C., seven hundred fires burned. In Chicago, white Mayor Richard Daley ordered police to shoot to kill arsonists and shoot to maim looters.

Perceiving (and in most cases misperceiving) their black neighbors as dangerous, millions of urban whites fled to the suburbs in the late 1960s and the 1970s. Detroit proper, which had boasted 1.85 million residents in 1950, saw its population dip to close to 1.2 million by the end of the 1970s.

Hundreds of people damage property and loot stores during a race riot in Detroit on July 23, 1967. (Courtesy of AP Images)

During that time, the city's white population dwindled from 84 percent to 36 percent. Since whites were typically more affluent than blacks, their departure left the cities with far less tax money.

In the 1970s, '80s, and beyond, many cities—Detroit, Cleveland, Washington, and others—became impoverished and rundown. City leaders invested in downtown areas but little else. Crime, drugs, and gangs were rampant. Kids needed to pass through metal detectors to enter their schools, which were woefully underfunded. While some urban blacks escaped the ghettos, the cycle of despair continued for most. In Cleveland in 1998, the high school dropout reached 72 percent—and much higher for males. At the dawn of the new century, more black men ages twenty to forty were in jail than in college.

Historian James P. Danky gave all Americans something to ponder when he stated:

> It is ironic that virtually every Martin Luther King Jr. Boulevard in America is a street of abandoned buildings, abandoned businesses, abandoned people, abandoned dreams. Those who honor King's name need to think about fulfilling the promise of his dream to those who have been forsaken in our inner cities.

In March 2005, thousands of Americans, black and white, converged on Selma to commemorate the fortieth anniversary of the 1965 march to Montgomery. U.S. Representative John Lewis (D-GA), who had co-led the Bloody Sunday march, helped organize the '05 event. Joining him were some forty members of Congress, Coretta Scott King (Martin Luther King's widow), and Lynda Johnson Robb (daughter of President Lyndon Johnson).

Marchers hold hands as they reenact the crossing of the Edmund Pettus Bridge on the fortieth anniversary of "Bloody Sunday." *(Courtesy of AP Images/Dave Martin)*

Visitors discovered a Selma that had changed much in forty years. The population remained about 20,000, but 70 percent of the city's residents were African American. Joseph Smitherman, who had served as mayor of Selma for all but one year from 1964 to century's end, had been unseated by African American James Perkins Jr. in 2000. Racial tension still existed in Selma, but Mayor Perkins said that residents had grown tired of talking about race problems. "I believe that most are ready to deal with strategies to make things better in spite of our individual or collective bias," he said.

The city of Selma commemorated its history with the National Voting Rights Museum, located near the Edmund Pettus Bridge. Moreover, in 1996 the U.S. Department of Transportation designated the Selma-to-Montgomery Scenic Byway an All-American Road.

Reenacting the historic march in 2005, demonstrators linked arms and sang freedom songs as they crossed the Edmund Pettus Bridge. The 10,000 who participated did so for various reasons. Some went to honor the heroes who had risked their jobs and lives by marching in 1965. "President Johnson signed that act," said Lewis, "but it was written by the people of Selma."

"This is a dream come true to be able to come across this bridge," said Shirley Patterson, who traveled fifteen miles to take part in the 2005 march. "In a way, it's kind of sad because I know people shed blood and died for the rights I have now. But I'm so proud to be here."

Marcher Scott Respress was equally moved. "More than anything, I'll remember the history, the great move forward from the past, the spiritual songs, and the heartfelt love," he said.

Faith and Politics President Doug Tanner added: "It's almost impossible not to get swept away in the emotional and spiritual power of making this pilgrimage. Particularly, making this journey with John Lewis is like traveling to the Holy Land with one of the Apostles."

The commemorative march also was a way to keep the spirit of the civil rights movement alive for young people. Said former NAACP Chairwoman Myrlie Evers-Williams: "It's a tragedy, really, that we find so many people who are unaware of that history. . . . It's our responsibility to be able to give them the background, that history, to help them relate it to today and to the future."

Tim Vickers, a student at Concordia College in Selma, was one young person who got the message. "I'm going to all of it," he said about the weeklong commemoration. "It's a big deal. By them getting voting rights, they changed the whole world."

In 2007, Congress voted to extend the Voting Rights Act of 1965 for another twenty-five years.

Section 5 of the Voting Rights Act requires certain southern states to have every voting change pre-cleared by the U.S. Justice Department. Some lawmakers feel that in the 21st century such a stipulation is excessive and unnecessary. Many disagree. The case of Dinwiddie County, Virginia, illustrates why. In the late 1990s, whites in Dinwiddie convinced the election supervisor to move the new polling place out of a black neighborhood and into a white area. The Justice Department felt the action showed "a discriminatory purpose," and it disallowed the move.

The issue of voting rights has been particularly salient in the 2000s. After George W. Bush barely won Florida over Al Gore to secure the 2000 presidential election, Democrats accused Republicans of disenfranchising Florida's black voters (who were mostly Gore supporters). Jesse Jackson and Florida Black Caucus members filed a lawsuit claiming that 16,000 votes were not counted in black inner-city neighborhoods in Duval County, Florida. Moreover, the NAACP compiled three hundred pages of testimony that included accusations of disenfranchisement in Florida, including voter intimidation and polling places in black neighborhoods being closed without notice. The governor of Florida was Jeb Bush, George's brother.

In 2004, President Bush defeated John Kerry in a hotly contested race that hinged on one swing state: Ohio. Ken Blackwell, the black Republican secretary of state of Ohio and a co-chair of the Bush election campaign, was accused of making unorthodox decisions to disenfranchise voters in Democrat-heavy (i.e., black) neighborhoods. For one thing, he refused to assign more than two voting machines (one of which was broken) in a heavily Democratic precinct. Some

The close presidential election of 2000 demonstrated the importance of every vote. Judge Robert Rosenberg, a canvassing board member, closely scrutinizes a disputed Florida ballot. *(Courtesy of AP Images/Wilfredo Lee)*

citizens in that precinct had to wait in line until 3 a.m. to vote; many others gave up and went home. Bush won Ohio 51 percent to 49 percent. If he had lost Ohio, Kerry would have won the election.

In those elections, Americans learned how important and precious each vote could be. They also realized that they could not take the right to vote for granted, that it was at least possible for politicians to cleverly prevent Americans from exercising their most basic right of citizenship. Prior to 1965, such disenfranchisement had occurred in the South on a massive scale. Only through the efforts of thousands of courageous Americans, who risked their jobs, bodily harm, and even their lives, did government finally correct the grievous injustice.

John Lewis, who suffered a fractured skull while leading the Bloody Sunday march, has returned to Selma to lead multiple commemorative marches. He has done so proudly. "[There] is nothing like walking across that bridge," he said. "Because on that bridge, some of us gave a little blood—to change America, to change America forever."

Timeline

1963–64		Attempts to end voting injustices in Selma, Alabama, fail.
1965	Jan. 2	Martin Luther King Jr. launches protest campaign against voting injustice in Selma.
	Jan. 18	King leads more than four hundred African Americans to Dallas County courthouse to register to vote; voters turned away.
	Jan. 19	Dallas County Sheriff Jim Clark assaults protester Amelia Boynton.
	Jan. 25	Demonstrator Annie Lee Cooper punches Jim Clark; Clark and his deputies pummel Cooper.
	Feb. 1	More than seven hundred protesters, including King and many children, arrested in Selma.
	Feb. 4	Federal judge outlaws Selma's voter registration tests and orders the city's registration board to speed up its registration

of black citizens; President Lyndon Johnson promises to secure voting rights for all citizens.

Feb. 9   King meets with President Johnson regarding voting rights.

Feb. 10   Jim Clark and his deputies impel more than a hundred teenage protesters on a forced march, making them run for three miles while being spurred with electric cattle prods.

Feb. 16   Jim Clark punches SCLC official C. T. Vivian outside the Dallas County courthouse.

Feb. 18   Jimmie Lee Jackson shot during a crackdown by Alabama state troopers; Jackson dies February 26.

March 5   Martin Luther King again discusses voting rights issues with President Johnson.

March 7   Six hundred marchers begin a trek from Selma to Montgomery; state troopers and local police attack marchers as they cross the Edmund Pettus Bridge; medical treatment required for dozens; day labeled "Bloody Sunday."

March 9   Martin Luther King leads 2,000 on a second march toward Montgomery; group prays and retreats rather than challenge the line of state troopers on Edmund Pettus Bridge;

angry whites attack three white ministers who participated in march; one, James Re[eb] from Boston, dies two days later on Marc[h]

March 13 President Johnson denounces the injusti[ce] in Alabama.

March 14 20,000 in Boston attend a memorial ser[vice] for James Reeb.

March 15 President Johnson requests the passage [of] a strict voting rights bill.

March 17 Federal Judge Frank M. Johnson rules t[hat] demonstrators are allowed to march fro[m] Selma to Montgomery.

March 20 President Johnson federalizes the Alaba[ma] National Guard to oversee the Selma to Montgomery march.

March 21–25 King leads a five-day march from Selm[a] to Montgomery; thousands participate i[n] the fifty-four-mile journey.

March 25 Some 25,000 demonstrators gather in Montgomery; white marcher, Viola Li[u] of Detroit, murdered by Ku Klux Klansm[an]

Aug. 3-4 The U.S. House of Representatives and the Senate pass the Voting Rights Act of 1965.

| Aug. 6 | The Voting Rights Act of 1965 signed by President Johnson. |

| Aug. 7 | U.S. Justice Department files suit against the use of the poll tax in Mississippi. |

| Aug. 10 | Examiners with the Civil Service Commission begin registering black citizens to vote in nine southern counties. |

The estimated number of registered black voters in Alabama rises from 111,000 in 1964 to 246,000.

More than seven hundred African Americans hold elected positions in the eleven southern states—nearly ten times more than in 1965.

Sources

CHAPTER ONE: White Voters Only

p. 10, "We want you . . ." Juan Williams, *Eyes on the Prize* (New York: Penguin Books, 1987), 264.

p. 10, "You can't keep . . ." Ibid., 264.

p. 13, "The power of granting . . ." Clayborne Carson, primary consultant, *Civil Rights Chronicle: The African-American Struggle for Freedom* (Lincolnwood, Ill.: Legacy Publishing, 2003), 185.

p. 13, "The problem in the South . . ." Henry Hampton and Steve Fayer, *Voices of Freedom* (New York: Bantam Books, 1990), 212.

CHAPTER TWO: Demanding The Ballot

p. 21, "hundreds of people . . ." Hampton and Fayer, *Voices of Freedom*, 213

p. 23, "the litigation method . . ." David J. Garrow, *Protest at Selma* (New Haven, Conn.: Yale University Press, 1978), 34.

p. 23, "The patience of the nation . . ." Ibid, 30.

p. 23-24, "They picked Selma . . ." Hampton and Fayer, *Voices of Freedom,* 216.

p. 24, "Jim Clark was . . ." Ibid., 214.

p. 25, "I propose that . . ." "President Lyndon B. Johnson's Annual Message to the Congress on the State of the Union: Jan. 4, 1965," Lyndon Baines Johnson Library and Museum, http://www.lbjlib.utexas.edu/johnson/archives. hom/speeches.hom/650104.asp.

p. 25-26, "If appeals to the state . . ." Matt Heron, "The March History: Voting Rights and Violence," http://www. takestockphotos.com/selma/violence.html.

p. 26-27, "charged that he [King]. . ." Taylor Branch, *Pillar of Fire* (New York: Simon & Schuster, 1997), 587.

p. 28, "She's an educated . . ." Jabari Asim, "Sunday, Bloody Sunday," *washingtonpost.com*, February 28, 2005, http://www.washingtonpost.com/wpdyn/articles/ A599372005Feb28.html.

p. 29, "Ain't nobody scared . . ." Chuck Stone, "Selma to Montgomery: The Road to Equality," *nationalgeographic. com,*http://www.nationalgeographic. com/ngm/0002/fngm/.

p. 30, "Clark whacked her . . ." Ibid.

p. 30, "They wrestled me . . ." Gil Klein and Michael Paul Williams, "Selma's 'Bloody Sunday' transformed the South," *TimesDispatch.com*, March 6, 2005, http://www.timesdispatch.com/servlet/Satellite?pagename =RTD/MGArticle/RT_BasicArticle&c=MGArticle&cid= 1031781381825.

p. 30, "If Negroes could . . ." Clayborne Carson, ed., *The Autobiography of Martin Luther King, Jr.* (New York: Warner Books, 1998), 275.

p. 32, "Why are we . . ." "A Letter from Martin Luther King from a Selma, Alabama Jail," *New York Times,* February 5, 1965.

p. 32, "may well show . . ." Paul Good, "Selma Drive Stepped Up By Negroes," *Washington Post,* February 4, 1965.

p. 33, "I hope that . . ." "Lyndon B. Johnson: 46-The President's News Conference of February 4th, 1965," American Presidency Project, Web site of John Woolley and Gerhard Peters at the University of California, Santa Barbara, http://www.presidency.ucsb.edu/ws/index.php?pid=27196.

p. 33, "You're making a mockery . . ." David J. Garrow, *Protest at Selma*, 56.

p. 33, "I had hoped . . ." Roy Reed, "Negroes in Selma Bar Voting Offer," *New York Times,* February 9, 1965.

p. 33, "The President made . . ." John D. Pomfrets, "President Promises Dr. King Vote Move," *New York Times,* February 10, 1965.

p. 34, "hide the demonstrators," Taylor Branch, *Pillar of Fire,* 586.

p. 34, "Move out! . . . didn't you?" Ibid., 586.

p. 34, "You wanted to march . . ." Ibid.

p. 36, "outside forces . . . breaking point," Ibid., 592.

p. 36, "Selma *still* isn't . . ." Ibid.

CHAPTER THREE: Bloody Selma

p. 38, "Then another white . . ." Hampton and Fayer, *Voices of Freedom,* 224.

p. 38, "beat people at random . . ." Steven Kasher, *The Civil Rights Movement: A Photographic History, 1954-68* (New York: Abbeville Press, 1996), 35.

p. 41, "Segregation now, segregation . . ." "Wallace Quotes," American Experience, *PBS.org*, 1963, http://www.pbs.

org/wgbh/amex/wallace/sfeature/quotes.html.

p. 42, "The patience of fair-minded . . ." *Associated Press*, February 28, 1965.

p. 42, "Oh, yeah . . ." Taylor Branch, *Pillar of Fire*, 599.

p. 43, "I must go see . . ." Ibid.

p. 43, "I had to preach . . ." Hampton and Fayer, *Voices of Freedom,* 226.

p. 44, "We will bring . . ." Taylor Branch, *Pillar of Fire*, 600.

p. 45, "I can't promise . . ." "The Central Points," *Time,* March 19, 1965, http://www.time.com/time/archive/ preview/0,10987,833543,00.html.

p. 46, "John, can you . . ." John Lewis, "Rep. John Lewis Commemorates the 40th Anniversary of the Voting Rights Act," Official Web site of Congressman John Lewis, August 3, 2005, http://www.house. gov/johnlewis/05pressreleases/pr080305.html.

p. 46, "This is an unlawful assembly . . ." David J. Garrow, *Protest at Selma,* 74.

p. 47, "May we have . . ." Roy Reed, "Alabama Police Use Gas and Clubs to Rout Negroes," *New York Times,* March 8, 1965.

p. 47, "Troopers, advance . . ." Ibid.

p. 48, "Tear gas! . . ." "The Central Points," *Time.*

p. 48, "O.K., nigger . . ." Ibid.

p. 48, "Fifteen or twenty nightsticks . . ." Reed, "Alabama Police Use Gas and Clubs to Rout Negroes," *New York Times,* March 8, 1965.

p. 49, "I was knocked . . ." *Ramparts,* June 1965.

p. 49, "One posseman tried . . ." Ibid.

p. 49-50, "I was blinded . . ." Sheyann Webb and Rachel

West Nelson, *Selma, Lord Selma,* (Tuscaloosa, Ala.: University of Alabama Press, 1980), 96.

p. 51, "They literally whipped . . ." Kasher, *The Civil Rights Movement,* 167.

p. 51, "Sheriff, keep your men . . ." "The Central Points," *Time..*

p. 51, "Get the hell out . . ." Ibid.

p. 51-52, "I don't see . . ." Reed, "Alabama Police Use Gas and Clubs to Rout Negroes," *New York Times,* March 8, 1965.

CHAPTER FOUR: "We Shall Overcome"

p. 53, "A shrill cry . . ." Kasher, *The Civil Rights Movement,* 168.

p. 53-54, "The violence in Selma . . ." Andrew Young, *An Easy Burden* (New York: HarperCollins, 1996), 358.

p. 54, "I fought in World . . ." Reed, "Alabama Police Use Gas and Clubs to Rout Negroes," *New York Times,* March 8, 1965.

p. 54, "We are here . . ." Hampton and Fayer, *Voices of Freedom,* 229-230.

p. 55, "legislation to guarantee . . ." "The Time Machine: 1965-Twenty-five Years Ago," *AmericanHeritage.com,* March 1990, http://www.americanheritage. com/articles/magazine/ah/1990/2/1990_2_34.shtml.

p. 55, "deplored the brutality . . ." "The Central Points," *Time.*

p. 57, "I have made . . ." Ibid.

p. 58, "We come to present . . ." Ibid.

p. 59, "back over the bridge . . ." Hampton and Fayer, *Voices of Freedom,* 231.

p. 60, "At least we had . . ." "The Central Points," *Time.*

p. 60, "northern Democratic liberals . . ." David J. Garrow, *Protest at Selma,* 89.

p. 61, "Ever since the events . . ." "Statement by President," *New York Times,* March 10, 1965.

p. 61, "best legal talent . . ." Ibid.

p. 61, "to approach this tense . . ." Ibid.

p. 64, "I abhor this . . ." "The Central Points," *Time.*

p. 65, "What you want . . ." Williams, *Eyes on the Prize,* 275.

p. 66, "In the meeting . . ." Hampton and Fayer, *Voices of Freedom,* 234.

p. 66, "What happened in Selma . . ." "Lyndon B. Johnson: 106-The President's News Conference on March 13th, 1965, "American Presidency Project, Web site of John Woolley and Gerhard Peters at the University of California, Santa Barbara http://www.presidency.ucsb.edu/ws/index.php?pid=26804.

p. 67, "Fight for freedom . . ." Carson, *The Sixties Chronicle,* 315.

p. 69, "Every American citizen . . ." "Special Message to the Congress: The American Promise," *C-SPAN.org,* http://cspan. org/executive/transcript.asp?cat=current_event&code=bush_admin&year= 365.

p. 70, "Open your polling places . . . "Ibid.

p. 70, "It is the effort . . ." Ibid.

p. 70, "When we heard . . ." Hampton and Fayer, *Voices of Freedom,* 236.

p. 71, "absolutely superb . . . the best ever," Horace Busby, "Voting Rights Message," Lyndon Baines Johnson Library and Museum, Office Files of White House Aides: Horace Busby, Box 3.

p. 72, "The law is clear . . ." "Selma-to-Montgomery March," National Park Service, http://www.cr.nps.gov/nr/travel/civilrights/al4.htm.

CHAPTER FIVE: The March

p. 73, "Recent events in Alabama . . ." Emmanuel Celler, ed., *Eigen's Political and Historical Quotations*, http://www.politicalquotes.org/Quotedisplay.aspx?DocID=15316.

p. 74, "I want my . . ." Roy Reed, "Alabama March Passes Midpoint," *New York Times,* March 24, 1965.

p. 75, "The scene inside . . ." *Nation,* May 10, 1965.

p. 75, "You will be the people . . ." Gary G. Yerkey, "Hard-won victory of civil rights revisited," *Christian Science Monitor,* March 7, 2005.

p. 77-78, "The final march . . ." Hampton and Fayer, *Voices of Freedom,* 236-237.

p. 78, "The March from Selma . . ." Ibid., 237-238.

p. 78, "I will never . . ." Ibid., 237.

p. 79-80, "I was much impressed . . ." Williams, *Eyes on the Prize,* 282.

p. 80, "Aren't you tired? . . ." Webb and Nelson, *Selma, Lord Selma,* 125-126.

p. 80, "An unemployed agitator . . ." "Protest on Route 80," *Time,* April 2, 1965.

p. 80, "evidence of much fornication . . .expectant mothers," Ibid.

p. 80, "We just had . . ." Williams, *Eyes on the Prize,* 282.

p. 81, "There never was . . ." "Our God Is Marching On!" *MLK Online,* http://www.mlkonline.net/ourgod.html.

p. 82, "Let us march . . ." Ibid.

p. 82, "prostitution of lawful process . . ." "Protest on Route 80," *Time,* April 2, 1965.   http://www.time.com/time/archive/preview/0,10987, 940994,00.html.

p. 83, "[Viola Liuzzo] was murdered . . ." "Lyndon B. Johnson: 135-The Televised Remarks Announcing the Arrest of Members of the Ku Klux Klan on March 26th, 1965, "American Presidency Project, Web site of John Woolley and Gerhard Peters at the University of California, Santa Barbarahttp://www.presidency.ucsb.edu/ws/index. php?pid=26836&st=viola+liuzzo&stl=

CHAPTER SIX: Breakthrough at the Ballot Box

p. 86, "I cherish that . . ." Gil Klein and Michael Paul Williams, "South was remade by ordeal in Selma," *TimesDispatch.com,* March 6, 2005, http://www. timesdispatch.com/servlet/Satellite?pagename= RTD/MGArticle/RT _BasicArticle&c=MGArticle&cid=1031781406078.

p. 86, "Today is a triumph . . ." "President Lyndon B. Johnson's Remarks in the Capitol Rotunda at the Signing of the Voting Rights Act: August 6, 1965," Lyndon Baines Johnson Library and Museum, http://www.lbjlib.utexas.edu/johnson/archives.hom/speeches.hom/650806.asp.

p. 86, "There are those . . ." Ibid.

p. 87, "Let me now say . . ." Ibid.

p. 92, "I was born . . ." "Dream of Things as They Ought to Be: Jesse Jackson, 1988," *Scholastic,* http://teacher. scholastic.com/researchtools/articlearchives/honormlk/spjackso.htm.

CHAPTER SEVEN: Life After Selma

p. 94, "sick and tired . . ." "Fannie Lou Hamer," *Encyclopedia Britannica Online*, http://www.britannica.com/ebi/article-9311572.

p. 95, "The only way . . ." Carson, *The Sixties Chronicle,* 275.

p. 95, "If America don't come . . ." Ibid., 326.

p. 97, "It is ironic . . ." Richard Newman, compiler, *African American Quotations* (New York: Facts on File, 2000), 267.

p. 98, "I believe that . . ." Gary G. Yerkey, "Hard-won victory of civil rights revisited," *Christian Science Monitor*, March 7, 2005.

p. 99, "President Johnson signed . . ." "Remembering Bloody Sunday," *Democracy Now!*, March 7, 2005, http://www.democracynow.org/article.pl?sid=05/03/07/1449252.

p. 99, "This is a dream . . ." Lance Griffin, "Local residents: Selma a solemn occasion," *Dothan Eagle,* March 7, 2005.

p. 99, "More than anything . . ." Ibid.

p. 99, "It's almost impossible . . ." Glenny Brock, "Monumental Concern," *Birmingham Weekly*, http://www.birminghamweekly.com/archived/pages/20050303_coverstory.php.

p. x99x, "It's a tragedy . . ." "Chronicle of The Civil Rights Era," *CBSNews.com*, February 18, 2004, http://www.cbsnews.com/stories/2004/02/17/earlyshow/leisure/books/main600823.shtml.

p. 99, "I'm going to all . . ." "Selma March marks 40 years, activists seek youth interest," *USA TODAY,* March 5, 2005, http://www.usatoday.com/news/nation/2005-03-05-selma-march-anniversary_x.htm?csp=34.

p. 102, "[There] is nothing . . ." "Remembering Selma," *TimesDispatch.com*, March 6, 2005, http://www. timesdispatch.com/servlet/Satellite?pagename=RTD/ MGArticle/RTD_BasicArticle&c=MGArticle&cid= 1031781381825.

Bibliography

Albert, Peter J., and Ronald Hoffman, eds. *We Shall Overcome*. New York: Da Capo Press, 1990.

American Experience. "Wallace Quotes." *PBS.org.,* 1963 (from his inaugural speech), http://wwwpbsorg/ wgbh/amex/wallace/sfeature/quotes.html.

Asim, Jabari. "Sunday, Bloody Sunday," *washingtonpost. com*, February 28, 2005, http://www.washingtonpost. com/wp-dyn/articles/A59937-2005Feb28.html.

Branch, Taylor. *Parting the Waters: America in the King Years, 1954-63*. New York: Simon and Schuster, 1988.

_____. *Pillar of Fire*. New York: Simon & Schuster, 1997.

Brock, Glenny. "Monumental Concern," *Birmingham Weekly*, http://www.birminghamweekly.com/archived/ pages/20050303_coverstory.php.

Bullard, Sara, ed. *Free at Last: A History of the Civil Rights Movement and Those Who Died in the Struggle*. Montgomery, Ala.: Southern Poverty Law Center, 1989.

Carson, Clayborne, ed. *The Autobiography of Martin Luther King, Jr.* New York: Warner Books, 1998.

———. David J. Garrow, Gerald Gill, Vincent Harding, and Darlene Clark Hine, eds. The *Eyes On the Prize*

Civil Rights Readers: Documents, Speeches, and Firsthand Accounts from the Black Freedom Struggle. New York: Penguin Books, 1987.

———. *Civil Rights Chronicle.* Lincolnwood, Ill: Legacy Publishing, 2003.

"Chronicle of The Civil Rights Era," *CBSNews.com.* February 18, 2004, http://www.cbsnews.com/stories/2004/02/17/earlyshow/leisure/books/main600823.shtml.

Fager, Charles. *Selma, 1965: The March That Changed the South.* Boston: Beacon Press, 1985.

Farber, David, cons. *The Sixties Chronicle.* Lincolnwood, Ill.: Legacy Publishing, 2004

Finlayson, Reggie. *We Shall Overcome: The History of t he American Civil Rights Movement.* Minneapolis: Lerner Publishing Group, 2002.

Gaillard, Frye. *Cradle of Freedom: Alabama and the Movement That Changed America.* Tuscaloosa, Ala.: University of Alabama Press, 2004.

Garrow, David J. *Bearing the Cross: Martin Luther King, Jr., and the Southern Christian Leadership Conference.* New York: Vintage Books, 1988.

_____. *Protest at Selma.* New Haven, Conn.: Yale University Press, 1978.

Good, Paul. "Selma Drive Stepped Up By Negroes." *Washington Post,* February 4, 1965,

Griffin, Lance. "Local residents: Selma a solemn occasion." *Dothan Eagle,* March 7, 2005, http://www.dothaneagle.com/servlet/Satellite?pagename=DEA/MGArticle/DEA_BasicArticle&c=MGArticle&cid=1031781418745&path=!frontpage.

Hampton, Henry, and Steve Fayer. *Voices of Freedom.* New York: Bantam Books, 1990.

Hudson, David M. *Along Racial Lines: Consequences of the 1965 Voting Rights Act.* New York: Peter Lang Publishing, 1998.

"Jesse Jackson, 1988: Dream of Things as They Ought to Be." *Scholastic.com* http://teacher.scholastic. com/researchtools/articlearchives/honormlk/ spjackso.htm.

Kasher, Steven. *The Civil Rights Movement: A Photographic History, 1954-68.* New York: Abbeville Press, 1996.

King Jr., Martin Luther. "A Letter from Martin Luther King from a Selma, Alabama Jail." *New York Times,* February 5, 1965.

Klein, Gil. "Voting Rights Act Up For Renewal." *TimesDispatch.com*, March 6, 2005, http://www. timesdispatch.com/servlet/Satellite?pagename= RTD/MGArticle/RTD_BasicArticle&c=MGArticle& cid=1031781382427.

Klein, Gil, and Michael Paul Williams. "Selma's 'Bloody Sunday' transformed the South," *TimesDispatch.com,* March 6, 2005, http://www. timesdispatch.com/servlet/Satellite?pagename= RTD/MGArticle/RTD_BasicArticle&c=MGArticle& cid=1031781381825.

Kotz, Nick. *Judgment Days: Lyndon Baines Johnson, Martin Luther King, Jr, and the Laws That Changed America.* Boston: Houghton Mifflin, 2005.

Lewis, John. "Rep. John Lewis Commemorates the 40th Anniversary of the Voting Rights Act." *United*

States House of Representatives, press release, August 3, 2005.

Newman, Mark. *The Civil Rights Movement.* Westport, Conn.: Praeger Publishers, 2004.

Newman, Richard, comp. *African American Quotations.* New York: Facts on File, 2000.

"Our God Is Marching On!" *MLK Online*, http://www. mlkonline.net/ourgod.html.

Pomfrets, John D. "President Promises Dr. King Vote Move." *New York Times,* February 10, 1965.

"President Lyndon B. Johnson's Remarks in the Capitol Rotunda at the Signing of the Voting Rights Act." *Lyndon Baines Johnson Library and Museum*, http://www.lbjlib.utexas.edu/johnson/archives. hom/speeches.hom/650806.asp.

"Protest on Route 80." *Time*, April 2, 1965.

Reed, Roy. "Alabama March Passes Midpoint." *New York Times,* March 24, 1965.

_____. "Alabama Police Use Gas and Clubs to Rout Negroes." *New York Times,* March 8, 1965.

_____. "Negroes in Selma Bar Voting Offer." *New York Times,* February 9, 1965.

"Remembering Bloody Sunday," *Democracy Now!,* March 7, 2005, http://www.democracynow.org/article.pl? sid=05/03/07/1449252.

"Remembering Selma." *TimesDispatch.com,* March 6, 2005, http://www.timesdispatch.com/servlet/Satellite? pagename=RTD/MGArticle/RTD_BasicArticle&c= MGArticle&cid=1031781381825.

"Selma March marks 40 years, activists seek youth interest." *USA Today,* March 5, 2005.

"Selma-to-Montgomery March." National Park Service,
U.S. Department of the Interior, http://www.cr.nps.
gov/nr/travel/civilrights/al4.htm.

Smiley, Tavis. *The Unfinished Agenda of the
Selma-Montgomery Voting Rights March.* Hoboken,
N.J.: John Wiley & Sons, 2005.

"Special Message to the Congress: The American
Promise." *C-SPAN.org.* http://c-span.org/
executive/transcript.asp?cat=current_event&code=bush_
admin&year=0365.

"Statement by President." *New York Times,* March 1
0, 1965.

Stone, Chuck. "Selma to Montgomery: The Road
to Equality," *nationalgeographic.com*, http://www.
nationalgeographic.com/ngm/0002/fngm/.

"The Central Points." *Time,* March 19, 1965.

"The March History: Voting Rights and Violence." *Take
Stock: Images of Change.* http://www.takestockphotos.
com/selma/violence.html.

Vaughn, Wally G., and Mattie Campbell Davis, eds. *The
Selma Campaign, 1963-1965.* Dover, Mass.: Majority
Press, 2005.

Webb, Sheyann, and Rachel West Nelson. *Selma, Lord
Selma.* Tuscaloosa, Ala.: University of Alabama Press,
1980.

Weisbrot, Robert. *Marching Toward Freedom 1957-1965.*
Broomall, Penn.: Chelsea House, 1994.

Wexler, Sanford. *Civil Rights Movement.* New York: Facts
on File, 1993.

Williams, Juan. *Eyes on the Prize*. New York: Penguin
    Books, 1987.
Yerkey, Gary G. "Hard-won victory of civil rights
    revisited," *Christian Science Monitor*,   March 7,
    2005.
Young, Andrew. *An Easy Burden*. New York:
    HarperCollins, 1996.

Web sites

http://www.lbjlib.utexas.edu/johnson/lbjforkids/main.htm
The Lyndon Baines Johnson Library and Museum has a special page on its official Web site for young readers. LBJ for Kids! features a Voting Rights Timeline, with a link to specific information about the Selma-to-Montgomery march. Visitors can read a series of letters written by Joseph Califano Jr. special assistant to the secretary of defense, outlining the progression of the march.

http://www.nps.gov/history/nr/travel/civilrights/al4.htm
This National Parks Service (NPS) Web site is a must-see. The NPS maintains the Selma-to-Montgomery National Historic Trail, and this site provides visitors with excellent background information. Follow the links to the "March Overview and Never Lose Sight of Freedom Edukit" page. There, you'll find interactive pages that feature people involved in the movement and a map to explore the location and events.

http://www.pbs.org/wgbh/amex/eyesontheprize/story/10_march.html
"I was hit in the head by a state trooper with a nightstick. . . . I thought I saw death." This quote by John Lewis, a leader in

the Student Nonviolent Coordinating Committee, is featured prominently on the opening page of this extensive PBS Web site on the "March from Selma to Montgomery, Alabama. March 1965." Other features include a sound recording of President Lyndon B. Johnson's "We Shall Overcome Speech," in support of the marchers, and a copy of a voter registration form designed to keep African Americans off the rolls.

Index